2/10

THE
BODY
LANGUAGE
HANDBOOK

How to
Read
Everyone's
Hidden
Thoughts
and
Intentions

6/9/10
Steve—
Here is a
valuable resource
for the
Provost's office!
You will be
an expert. :)

my best
wishes as
you begin
this new
adventure at
L.S.U. You
will do
well —
Sandy

GREGORY HARTLEY AND
MARYANN KARINCH

CAREER
PRESS
Franklin Lakes, NJ

D0763441

THE BUSINESS TREE
EDITED BY JODI BRANDON
TYPESET BY EILEEN MUNSON
Cover design by Howard Grossman/12E Design

To order this title, please call toll-free 1-800-CAREER-1 (NJ and Canada: 201-848-0310) to order using VISA or MasterCard, or for further information on books from Career Press.

The Career Press, Inc., 3 Tice Road, PO Box 687,
Franklin Lakes, NJ 07417
www.careerpress.com

Library of Congress Cataloging-in-Publication Data

CIP Data available upon request.

To my brother and best friend,
Mike Hartley.
Everyone should be so lucky
to have as good a friend as you.

—*Greg Hartley*

To Mom,
Karl,
and Jim
with love and gratitude.

—*Maryann Karinch*

Acknowledgments

First, thanks to our wonderful candid models: Tony Garibay, Kurtis Kelly, Brittany Kimel, Greg Parker, Jodi Clawson, Carla Story, Kim Alexander, Brian Cooper, Austin Cooper, Tyler Cooper, Megan Salomone, and Kofi Nti. Maryann has been a wonderful writing partner for this—our sixth book together. Michael Pye at Career Press has been ultimately flexible and helpful in the process of creating and putting this book together; thanks for understanding. Bigstock Photo provided wonderful photos for this book; visit their Website to see the names of gifted photographers who contribute to their catalog. A handful of lifelong friends have always been there, Walt, Max, Collins, and Nellums, to always remind me of where I come from and to be there regardless of change—thanks.

Thanks especially to Jim McCormick for agreeing to play along and support the body language book by modeling, being a sane voice in the wilderness that provides me with optimism, and, more importantly, a friend.

Finally, thanks to the American Fighting Men and Women, who serve to protect the constitution of the United States, for putting themselves in harm's way in support of decisions made by our elected officials with little input to the process.

—Greg Hartley

My thanks to Greg. Our adventure together of six books has been fun and a tremendous learning experience for me. I join him in thanking our models and the photographers at Bigstock. Much appreciation to my partner and friend, Jim McCormick; I agree with Greg that he's a good sport and a sane voice. Sincere appreciation to the team at Career Press. These are folks who provide support from the moment a project gets started to the years after it's published: Michael Pye, Laurie Kelly-Pye, Kirsten Dalley, Gina Talucci, Diana Ghazzawi, Karen Roy, Jodi Brandon, Adam Schwartz, Allison Olsen, Ron Fry, and others behind the scenes. I also want to thank my mother, brother, and friends for their continuing interest in my work. And thanks to my professors at the Catholic University of America Speech and Drama Department. It turns out that an excellent education in acting provides a good foundation for the study of body language.

—Maryann Karinch

Ev'ry little movement has a meaning all its own,
Ev'ry thought and feeling by some posture can be shown,
And ev'ry love thought that comes a stealing
O'er your being
Must be revealing.

From "Every Little Movement" by Otto Harbach,
renowned Broadway lyricist and librettist,
with permission of William O. Harbach

Contents

How to Use This Book

This handbook will help you read body language and use it intentionally to create effect. Learning to do both involves both science and art. On the science side, you have physiology, psychology, social science, anthropology—and that's just for starters. On the art side, you have physiognomy and the need to observe how pieces come together—the interaction of body movements, nuances, coloration and determined by culture, context, and relationships.

The reason you want to read through the entire handbook at least once before you skip to case studies and lists to get answers is that you need the background in both the science and the art to interpret what you see in an individual person. If you simply match movements with meanings, you will get it right only occasionally. But by familiarizing yourself with why people make certain movements, how they make them, and how you can determine when something is intentional or unintentional, you can frequently get it right—with practice.

The Introduction will give you important background in primate non-verbal communication and help you eliminate the junk ideas about body language you've picked up throughout the years from pop psychology—that is, the instant interpretations that are often wrong.

Chapter 1 gives insights about nature and nurture, with an in-depth look at the five factors of nurture that affect human communication. You get to know yourself better through this information, and that helps you understand how the five factors surface in other people and affect their communication. You will see how these factors affect both intentional and unintentional messaging.

Chapter 2 covers involuntary and universal body language, so you go deeper into the unintentional signaling and the facial expressions and types of movements that human beings have in common. You get a good look at the Big Four—illustrators, regulators, barriers, and adaptors—and that discussion provides information that will apply again and again as you develop your interpretive skills as well as your ability to use body language proactively.

Chapter 3 introduces you to the impact of culture on non-verbal communication. You see dramatic illustrations of how projection gets people into unpleasant or even dangerous situations: In short, when you assume that a particular gesture means something because it means something in your culture, you are no longer in a position to understand the real message. This chapter also covers the limits of expression imposed by the brain and body.

By the time you arrive at the head-to-toe scans of individual movements and non-language sounds in chapters 4 through 8, you are ready to start applying skills of interpretation rather than just memorizing movement-message connections. This is the difference between flipping to the chapters on individual elements of body language, or to the case studies, and understanding what's behind the information. It's the value of having the handbook progress to the information. Among other things, you easily see how movements combine as illustrators, or what serves as a barrier in one situation and a regulator in another, as well as the relative significance of movements of different parts of the body; you have a developing sense of what single movement might trump another, and what unintentional movements are giving the real message, regardless of what else might be going on.

As you look into reviewing the holistic view of understanding body language, you have then arrived at the point where you can identify behaviors, moods, and underlying messages with some regularity. The case studies in Chapter 9 plunge you into the practical and explicit interpretation of the body language of individuals as they relate to one another and leak hidden messages in different environments.

Fundamental skills that develop throughout the course of the chapters are the ability to sort intentional non-verbal communication from unintentional and perceiving the effect of relationships on body language. Whether you are in control, under someone else's control, or in a position of equality or compromise makes a difference in the way behaviors are manifested. And in every analysis you make, you learn the importance of knowing someone's baseline, or how an individual acts in a relatively low-stimulus environment.

Baseline body language is what is normal for a person—that is, the natural surfacing of all of nature and nurture influences in the way someone sounds and moves. As people go through life, we tend to develop idiosyncrasies that other people read meaning into because they don't do them. But they are part of the baseline—part of what constitutes "normal" for an individual.

As a matter of course in reading body language, you will make note of the difference between normal and deviation from normal for the person you are trying to read. That is how you see the hidden messages leak out. It is how you see the lies, love, confusion, and real danger.

Just remember: This is a body language book, not an ESP book. You can use it to perceive messages other people are sending, whether they mean to or not, but that doesn't mean you can use the information here to read someone's mind.

Carry the book around with you and watch how people respond when they realize you have begun cultivating an expertise in reading body language. Take it with you to meetings as you refresh your knowledge of how to use body language proactively to influence others. Enjoy the rich experience of understanding the signals people around you are constantly emitting.

Introduction

Humans are primates with a million words to help us express exactly what we mean. Other primates communicate effectively without words—even though they could use words if they wanted to. Research in the late 1990s at Georgia State University's language research center demonstrated that fact with a pygmy chimp who used words with scientists and taught them to her own son. Years earlier, zoologist Desmond Morris (*The Naked Ape*) observed that primates who had learned a few words dropped that form of communication when researchers stopped goading them to use it.

Rather than rely on words, non-human primates use a system of active body language signals to communicate messages. These intentional signals can range from the waving of limbs to facial expressions to posturing. The alpha in the primate world clearly demonstrates his intended message: "Come here." "Go away." "That female is mine and I will beat you into the ground if you touch her." This active posturing and message-sending has been passed on by our common primate ancestors to us. Most of this intentional body language is coarse and universally understood. Some modern non-human primates might teach each other new signals that pass from generation to generation within a collective, but all primates of the same species recognize basic intentional signaling without training.

There is a much more subtle version of this body language communication than all of the intentional noise and flailing associated with being alpha. It is the ability to read the seemingly insignificant cues that are unintentional. When you are less than alpha in the chimp world, you have either been born there or fallen to that rank. There are no courts to right your wrongs, and retribution is swift and harsh for any violation of the alpha's authority. Any chimp wanting to rise in rank, or stay out of the alpha's path, needs to understand the wishes of the alpha before those wishes involve violence—and often before the alpha is even aware he is signaling. This same principle reaches across most of the communal animal kingdom: Understanding body language has its rewards.

The early active body language our primitive ancestors shared was easily understood by all but the most inept among them. The most rudimentary communication was easy to recognize. There are few examples of universally understood body language within our species today, but you can still see the remnants. Even from a distance, most humans can easily recognize tenderness, rage, and fear. The signs are evident and tied to daily survival.

Place your balled fists in front of you with palms facing inward; move them up and down in a pounding action. What does this signify? For most of us, it demonstrates rage, anger, or at least dissatisfaction. No one needs to teach you this. Much like our ape kin, we understand it to be a declaration of thoughts.

Along the human evolutionary path, we made great divergences from our ape kin. Although our vocal organs do not differ significantly from chimpanzees', our desire to be understood differs dramatically.

As we evolved toward increasingly more communicative beings, simply using ubiquitous body language no longer sufficed. We wanted to get our *exact* point across, to have the nuances be easily understood. Listen to a human baby before he masters the spoken language of his parents: He has his own spoken language as he tries to communicate. No one else might understand his gibberish, but he seems convinced that he is clearly making his point. As our human ancestors began developing spoken language, they must have felt as frustrated as that baby.

How does a group of people develop a common language? Think about how you, as an adult, try to learn a foreign language. You need the capability to equate a given word to another word in order to have meaning. This is part of the reason adults have such a hard time with foreign languages. We try to associate a word like *beit* (Arabic) for the English word *house*. When a young child is learning a language he is creating labels for items, not exchanging one word for another. He is assigning new labels all the time, so which language they come from is unimportant. A 2-year-old child does not care about constructing grammatically correct sentences. The important thing is that you understand what he means.

Assigning these labels to new objects is easy. A person can point to the object and speak the label. "Me Tarzan—You Jane" is a classic example of this. But what happens when the word represents an action instead of an object? Or when visual stimulus is not an option? If you have enough words you negotiate your way to a common understanding of the concept. This negotiation of language is common with second languages and is why so many first-year language students learn "how do you say…?" in their target languages. The next level of sophistication is to act out the word that you want in the new language. For example, you do not know the word for the thing you use to unlock the door, so you mimic turning a key. This sophisticated negotiation of language separates successful students of foreign language from those who repeat school-taught phrases and words. A common language is an evolving tool produced by all parties involved.

After we developed spoken language, we had entirely new sets of symbols to communicate mood, intent, and desires. By its very nature, the development of words meant that human speech would become a tribal commodity that allowed each tribe to understand other members and insulated communication from the outside. That language could only stay universal by constant interface between its speakers.

Whether you take the Old Testament literally or believe it to be a series of ancient religious myths, the story of the Tower of Babel clearly illustrates the power of common language. Up to that point in the Bible, everyone spoke a common language, which enabled them to decide to build a stairway to heaven jointly. God easily disturbed this self-aggrandizing effort by causing them to speak differently, preventing them from cooperating to complete the project.

Take a reversed approach to the Tower of Babel story, and assume a pre-existence of disparate and confusing communication symbols. The new story is this: Leadership of a newly formed kingdom in ancient times wants to build a tower to reach the heavens. These ancient and dissimilar humans have orders to work together to accomplish the grand goal of building a stairway to heaven. As each supervisor tries to communicate using his tribe's version of the word *here*, he gets really frustrated with the stupid villagers from the other tribes. Only when he acts out the action of placing a block in a given location (ubiquitous body language mimicry) can the other villagers slightly understand that *huna* means *here*. Soon the shared lexicon begins to be the language of that group of workers. That does not make the lexicon universal for others; it simply creates a new language for the tribe that is the construction crew on the tower. Spoken language allows a group to define clearly a subset of body language to replace spoken word. As spoken language becomes universal on the tower, the workers can create a new system of non-spoken language in gesture to illustrate the same concepts from a distance and over noise. The gestures have one key element in common: They are universally agreed on and understood by both parties communicating. The hand signals can communicate "I need four laborers and a mason here" even from a distance.

This becomes the language of the tower project only, and any outsider who shows up might still confuse what he sees or hears. With human beings, language is contagious. As each of these workers returns to his hut in the evening he unintentionally infects others with new vocabulary words. He says to his wife, "Come huna," and he might even use new "gestures" instinctively to get his point across.

In typical human fashion, the workers' families develop their own versions of the workers' tongue, and before you know it most of the villagers have a sort of trade language. The gesturing and the spoken language allow all of the villagers to communicate to a greater degree than before. This group has now created an insulating core of spoken and body language that is not clear to outsiders.

Then one day the unthinkable happens. A new ruler kills the project and there is no work for the villagers. The villagers scatter to the ends of the earth looking for work. The common tongue they all shared is less than useless—it's disruptive in their new lands. And they now have to learn a third language. At every turn, they look for others who seem to understand them and who are initiated as speakers of the trade language or anything that sounds remotely familiar. They are drowning in misunderstandings and clinging to anything that keeps them afloat. As they try to use familiar signals and words, they look constantly for someone who understands. One day, they simply give up on using the old trade language. Some of the old words and actions die harder than others because, just like spoken words, gestures carry connotation as well as denotation. If their repertoire includes a gesture the ruling class had used to demean a laborer, that's one that will die hard because of the emotion associated with it.

And then, one afternoon, one of the tower workers sees someone who wasn't from his group using that old familiar gesture used to demean him back during the days of construction. It brings back to the surface all of the same meaning it had before. He reacts. The problem is it means something dramatically different in his new place and at this new time.

A Holistic Look

Messaging by any person is complex because we each send a complete set of signals composed of both intentional and unintentional actions. When we are angry, we might well send a mix of intentional signals of dissatisfaction and unintentional signals about our insecurity in the matter. For that reason, one simple rule applies to reading body language: There are no simple rules.

Human communication is a mosaic. Even if you purchase thousands of dollars worth of equipment, set up a laboratory, and study every person you meet like a lab rat, you'll probably only come close to 100 percent certainty about what someone means. Body language is an art form, and every person is a different canvas. Just like choice of words, pronunciation style, and rate of speech make every person's voice different, many factors affect body language. You need to learn about the canvas the person's body language is painted on—that is, you need to baseline to understand what something really means. Sometimes a scratch is a reaction to a mosquito bite, and sometimes it's a sign of distress.

Cognates and Universally Understood Body Language

Take what you do know and analyze this photo. In this case, there is no right or wrong answer. Just make a record of what you see. Later in the book, we will analyze this photo piece by piece so you will get the real story.

What do you think this man is communicating?

a) Anger.

b) A demand.

c) Emphasis on a point.

d) Excitement.

Do you have any thoughts about the message driving the action?

What does his posture mean?

What about those closed eyes?

While his right hand is doing something, what is his left hand doing?

There is one key piece of information you need to know about the canvas. This man is from Ghana, and, in his part of Ghana, this gesture signals food. He is happily demonstrating this and leaning forward in the chair to share with the photographer. As he says, the signal, which has tremendous connotation in his culture, is derived from a time when food came from the pounding of rootstock to create flour. So while he is actually asking you to break bread, his signal might be clearly misinterpreted by someone without a common language or culture and no way to negotiate meaning. By the way, his eyes are closed because the winder on the camera caught him in mid-blink.

Just like the scattered tower workers, we look for commonly understood words and gestures. But because these gestures are not understood by others, they fall on blind eyes or worse. Using gestures that others do not understand is like swearing at fish: It might make you feel better but the fish will not understand. Plus, you might look foolish to the non-fish.

That potential for embarrassment has not stopped both unseasoned and seasoned travelers from making similar mistakes around the globe. People often forget that gestures are not ubiquitous and that false cognates extend from spoken language into the realm of body language. So as the traveler realizes he is not communicating effectively, he starts to negotiate with body language instead of words. Gestures are profoundly meaningful; they are part of most people's intentional communications strategy and come to the surface as freely as words. Because neither has a common foundation, the gestures only compound the confusion.

False Cognates in Body Language

A British diplomat went through an Arabic language course a friend of mine taught. His wife had the opportunity to take an abbreviated version of the course, too, before they both went to Yemen.

One feature of Arabic is that it has no "p" sound, so whenever an English word is pronounced with an Arabic accent the "p" turns to a "b." The wife learned enough Arabic so that she could say things like "I want" and "I need" followed by some common nouns.

Her husband broke the zipper on his pants and she decided to go to the local tailor and ask for a replacement so she could do the repair herself. She intended to say, "I want a zipper," but realized she didn't know the word for it so she said "zibber," which is the phonetic spelling of the Arabic word for penis. When he kept asking her to repeat her request, she became adamant and began unzipping her pants. Good body language for trying to communicate what she 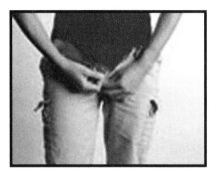 wanted—if she hadn't already suggested that she wanted something else that shared the same signal. Keep that story in mind when you think you're sending the same message with your words and body language. You may not be.

Because you probably want to know what happened, I'll finish the story. The man went to the neighboring store to get a friend, just to have witness to the fact that this beautiful blonde woman was asking him for sex. The man happened to speak English fairly well and quickly translated—much to the tailor's dismay, I am sure.

Can We Ever Really Understand Each Other?

If body language is as fraught with double meaning and false cognates as two unrelated languages, then how can we apply rules of body language to humans in any fashion?

When you are talking about spoken words and gestures—actions that have an agreed-upon meaning within a group—you are watching the human equivalent of a chimp signaling and howling. His language is intentional; the expression is supposed to convey a certain message. Although there are exceptions, these actions are part of language under the conscious control of the messenger. Because humans want so desperately to be understood and have evolved into highly communicative beings, much more subtle communication strategies are at work as well. Some sounds and movements can only be controlled by the most adept practitioners of the art of body language. Others are so commonplace that people around you use them all the time, but most likely you do not even notice them.

The Challenges Here and Now

Humans are wonderfully vocal primates with a drive to communicate like no other primate. We develop and retire languages across the ages based on replacement by new and more useful ones. In learning to read body language, you have to go through a process of muting the vocal expressions that have blunted your senses to perceive all of the other types of language. Now that English officially has one million words, we officially have one million ways to reduce our reliance on the senses.

The very technologies that help us cultivate communication with language can exacerbate the problem. As you sit in a room or cubicle and interact with people electronically, you may be putting your ability to read body language to sleep. Until there is a more multisensory version of the Internet than Web 2.0 (the one-millionth word, by the way), we will rely on emoticons and text for a lot of our messaging.

Even though human beings are designed to use and read body language—an aspect of us that gives us a common bond with our primate ancestors—we are typically on a bell curve in terms of the ability to understand it. Some people are born with a limited ability or lack of ability to read body language. They have to learn it just as you would have to learn the vocabulary and rules of another language if you suddenly moved to a country where your native language wasn't spoken.

In the case of people with Asperger's Syndrome, for example, language skills appear fine, but the condition affects the ability to read gestures and perceive social conventions. After Maryann and I wrote *I Can Read You Like a Book*, someone wrote an Amazon.com review that affected us, and affected this book: "I had an unusual reason to order this book—my child has a mild case of Asperger's Syndrome. This means that she lacks the skills to interpret body language unless she learns it as a 'second language.' So I bought it with her in mind. As I read it, I was surprised how extremely helpful it was for ME. I honestly never realized how much I was missing! The skills it teaches will help with relationships of all kinds, business and personal."

I'm not citing this to slip in an endorsement; I just want you to see that understanding basic body language cannot be something we take for granted.

Contrast an individual with Asperger's with someone like Frank Abagnale, the gifted imposter who now consults with the Federal Bureau of Investigation and other law-enforcement entities. His ability to read people and project competence—even as a teenager—enabled him not only to pass millions of dollars' worth of bad checks, but also to gain acceptance as a pilot, physician, and lawyer. No one taught him those body language skills, so his ability is as natural as the inability of someone with Asperger's to perceive acceptance or rejection and everything in between.

Most of us fall somewhere in between the two extremes, but, no matter where you are on the bell curve, you can use this handbook to get better. As humans, we blunt our ability to read body language by relying heavily on written communication, especially texting and other "instant" forms of getting a message across, to the extent that we don't even see each other in the physical, tangible sense. The popularity of TV shows featuring body language experts or expertise suggests that people feel that reading body language gives them an edge. It's no longer an ability that everyone has to some extent; it's an art-science hybrid that many think must be learned.

In trying to learn body language, you probably find yourself looking for formulas. There is only one: work to understand the individual. One move does not always mean "I trust you," or another always mean "Go away!" The first question I would like you to address as you move to Chapter 1 is: What do crossed arms really mean?

The answer is likely the first of many surprises about body language you will encounter in these pages.

What Do YOU Mean by That?

When people ask me "What is the most common mistake people make in interpreting body language?" I think of the story of the blind men and the elephant. Each man must describe the elephant—a completely foreign creature to all of them—by touching only one part.

When you conclude after a glance at someone's crossed arms or half-smile that you know what that individual is communicating, you're like one of the blind men. Your fragment of an idea could get you close to the big picture, but it's more likely that your conclusion is far from accurate.

Learning the art and science of interrogation to serve in any environment, military or law enforcement, involves cultivation of an ability to see intent. In training interrogators, I have taught them to look at a person holistically to see how word and deed come together in a particular context.

How do you get to a point where you understand intent—that is, what a person is really communicating? First, you have to understand how he communicates. The developmental factors of nature and nurture provide the basic clues.

» **Nature:** Genetics play a fundamental role in how we express ourselves. After decades of observation, I'm convinced we are predisposed to certain types of communication. Whether we are loud or quiet, forceful or contained, to some extent the communication that "comes naturally" really is natural for us. There is just a whole lot stuck in our heads that has to do with biology. We have the capacity to transform or overcome it—a little or a lot—but we do come with predispositions.

  ▶▶ Physical attributes: There are ways you can move your joints that I can't move mine, and ways I can move my forehead that you probably can't move yours. And those are just superficial examples of what constitute a complex array of possible differences linked to our physiology.

  ▶▶ Energy: Your natural energy level shows up in how much you like to move, your metabolism, and the speed and power you put into your communication. You can alter it artificially—watch a little kid after eating a candy bar—and you can alter it through habits, but your body has a natural level that affects your behavior. Much of the challenge of reading body language is linked to perceiving deviations from the norm or baseline in energy level.

» **Nurture:** The people who train you in using body language, whether formally or informally, could be your family, teachers, neighbors, and Big Bird on *Sesame Street*. Role models also affect your expression; you do what they do because you admire them, whether consciously or on a subconscious level. All of these people help cultivate your development in five areas that directly affect how you communicate:

▶ Self-awareness.

▶ Sophistication.

▶ Personal style, or grooming.

▶ Situational awareness.

▶ A sense of others' entitlement and what is proper.

Focus on Nurture

An in-depth look at the five factors of communication style spotlights what comes out of nurturing that profoundly affects your body language. After that, I take you through the ways those factors develop so you can better track what happened to you, and how you might be affecting the next generation.

Self-Awareness

A friend's 8-year-old son displayed unbridled enthusiasm about being at the rodeo with his dad. He jumped around screaming, not caring what anybody thought of him. Just for the heck of it, he went over to an iron gate and put his head through the bars. Claustrophobia quickly set in. He flailed and screamed as people walking by laughed at him. After he got his head out, everybody who walked by him and smiled or laughed got him upset. He would get mad and try to go at them, even though they weren't laughing at him or about him. In his mind, everyone who passed him with a look of amusement had to be making fun of him. In five minutes, he went from behavior that showed no self-awareness to behavior that showed acute self-awareness.

In general, the more self-aware you are, the less likely you are to broadcast information intentionally. You will control your hands in a job interview no matter how nervous you are, for example. But just as in a continuum of any kind, as you keep moving more and more to the extreme you find yourself manifesting the same behavior as someone on the other end of the continuum. Too much self-awareness, therefore, makes you less in touch with what you're broadcasting. You expend so much energy and focus on self-awareness that emotions leak out involuntarily.

Sophistication

Sophistication is a two-pronged factor: first, understanding exactly where you fit in the hierarchy and what that means in terms of how you *should* communicate; second, understanding enough about your signaling through body language to know what a given piece of body language means. Only then can you know enough to fit into society and match your expression to that understanding. You know what your point is and can get it across to the audience in front of you. People who lack sophistication use the same signals and images with every audience and expect to get the same responses from them. Small children who only ever communicate with their parents find themselves saying and doing things that other adults may find incomprehensible. This is an extreme example of a lack of sophistication.

A friend had two daughters. One had intelligence and sophistication; she taught high school. The other had physical beauty; she was a stripper. The first had a keen sense of how people perceived her and how to treat them, but her appearance and movements suggested she had very little self-awareness. Her sister was intensely self-aware; she put herself together well and knew how to send messages with her movements. She was oblivious about how people perceived her—to the point where it was a joke. Think of the caricature of the dumb-blonde gun moll from a 1940s movie and you get the picture.

Personal Style

You might also call this grooming. As you grow up, people reinforce certain of your behaviors and discourage others in an effort to polish your body language.

All of us start off in life as little savages—some to a greater and some to a lesser degree, depending on predisposition. If society and interaction with adults and psychological development did not curtail that unrestrained activity, those of us who survived would eventually turn into very strong toddlers with one desire: whatever struck our fancy at the moment. Along the way, nurture and psychological development temper how we respond to a given situation. As culture evolves so does the way we as individuals respond. Small Southern children of the past addressed all adults as Sir or Ma'am, and Mister or Miss. Even among the poorest and least-educated Southerners a child who overheard his parent call a friend Bill would use this same familiar term, and the parent would correct the child: "That's Mister Bill to you." This behavior was so ubiquitous in the South that even the most unpolished children always spoke to adults with deference.

The same patterns hold true for other cultures as well, whether in the United States or another country. Acceptable behavior is entrenched in each of us as a child by those who serve as role models. Of course, each of these role models is sending messages based on her past role models, self-awareness, and sophistication, so the complexity is enormous. We have teachers, clergy, peer groups, mentors, bosses, and even television characters to assist along the way. What was normal for the American South was very different from what was normal for Sister Mary Katherine in the northeast. As a consequence, children reared in the conservative Baptist South and children reared in the conservative Roman Catholic North had very different social norms. Just like the workers in the Tower of Babel village, if left to their own devices parents could dilute the behavior and create whole new social norms within their own domain. Fortunately (and unfortunately) parents are not the only role models to impact or groom us.

As Baby Boomers have matured in an age of globalized economy and social structure, and interstate migration has changed the face of the South among all strata of society, those old norms and social trends have disappeared to the point that it sounds odd to me today to be called Mister Greg by a young child. Each culture creates acceptable standards for behavior. As we meld cultures across the United States, these cultural norms meld as well. Each of the interactions we have from childhood to death is constantly changing our personal style as we are groomed to behave in new ways.

Situational Awareness

The first three factors can easily fit into a style of individual skills. Situational awareness relies heavily on how the person pays attention to an outside stimulus or what is going on around him and how he fits in the situation. Situational awareness has a profound effect on sophistication, primarily because it can be situation-dependent— that is, easily displaced in a person who is not fluid in moving from one situation to the next.

A savvy person can spend her entire life in a few square blocks of a large city and understand every nuance of the local culture. While she is in this area she is keenly aware of everything that goes on around her; she has a sophisticated view and situational awareness. At the same time, a person living in a rural area or small country town is doing precisely the same thing with his local group. Both are keenly aware of their situations for the same reasons, but with different invitational signals and different warnings. But although their insular views of what body language is appropriate might make them sophisticated in their limited environments, they show a complete lack of situational awareness in the world at large. A young person growing up in a relatively cloistered community of any kind—Hasidim, Amish, Wiccan, polygamous Mormon—could inadvertently send signals to the outside that are dangerous to the prosperity, if not the life, of the people who live within the community.

Take any of these people out of his environment and place him into a new venue. His success hinges on how adeptly he grasps the signals of his new group and how well he overcomes the insecurity of being out of his element. Situation comedies rely heavily on the attempt to make this transition.

People are all over the spectrum in terms of sensing where they fit in any given group, much the way they are in reading body language or in sophistication. This can be represented on a bell curve. At one extreme end, you have a person oblivious to changes and the situation around her; she thinks and acts as though Manhattan, a borough of New York City, and Manhattan in the state of Kansas are the same. At the other extreme is the superbly aware person who notices subtle nuances of culture and signaling wherever she goes.

An individual's understanding of where and how he fits is only the first part. The companion piece is how he reacts. He may simply relax and feel comfortable in his own skin, regardless of what surprises ensue. Or, he may try so hard to fit in that he alienates others with the effort. What happens when inordinate effort goes into either process can be represented on a radial diagram: Go too far in one direction, and, eventually, you loop around and end up at the other extreme. In other words, the result of being too cool or not cool enough can result in alienation of people around you.

Either extreme indicates high situational awareness and low sophistication. But when a person maintains a centered approach of using what she knows and attempting to be understood, she displays high situational awareness and high sophistication.

A Sense of Others' Entitlement and What Is Proper

This factor depends a great deal on interaction with people outside your little world as you develop psychologically. If you only have a sense of other people's entitlement in a homogenous community, then you don't know what is proper beyond that environment. Your sense of others' entitlement is also highly dependent on situational awareness; it's last in the list of factors because it reflects a build of one factor on the next.

A person who is raised to know everything there is to know about the ways of refined people, who understands all of the rules of the country club, and who is keenly aware of the cues coming at her in the most elite of settings might still be lacking in a sense of others' entitlement. If her normal behavior includes shortchanging "the help" in their entitlements, then she is likely to signal that body language to "the help." And street-savvy people who treat those who can't navigate around the city as morons lack a sense of others' entitlement as well. Their treatment of people who don't "know the ropes" matches the demeaning nature of people who don't respect "the help." Melodramas, fables, and other stories play heavily on the archetypes of someone who has everything in a particular environment and yet needs something that only someone from across town can provide.

Someone keenly aware that other people have rights will demonstrate insecurity when she steps on those rights; only through practice can a person learn to mask that insecurity. A person who has no belief in the rights or entitlement of others will walk rudely on those she does not value.

In a scene from the movie *Braveheart*, King Edward has forced infantry troops into battle with the Scots. When the battle goes poorly, Edward orders the commander to have archers fire. The commander balks. He wonders: If we do that, won't we hit our own men, too? Edward acknowledges that's true—but the enemy's men will also get hit, so the assault should proceed. Someone lacking a sense of others' entitlement will demonstrate behavior that focuses on the end at all costs, not the means.

Chemistry and Judgment

Nature involves the voice and the tone you are given. You can stretch the tone to be clearer, and train the voice to grow stronger and do marvelous things. Acknowledge the limits of nature, though: You have little impact on the vocal cords you were born with. If you were not born to sing opera well, you won't sing opera well.

Each of the five factors has an impact on signaling and on receiving. Each of them is a part of your past based on experiences of nurture rather than nature. Think about your life and how very different your exact experiences are from anyone else you know. You might share memories of events with a group of friends, but your memories are slightly different from theirs. Similar to the worker at the Tower of Babel who shares a common language and gestures, and then gets ripped from the commonality, when we have experienced something significant in our past, it leaves a mark. These factors combine and compound not only to affect how we signal someone else, but also to leave impressions. There are meanings attached to movements, and preconceptions about what another person is saying.

Reality TV shows are replete with examples of people willing to walk on stage and demonstrate poor situational awareness and no sophistication by singing loudly and badly.

When you see that, think of how most people understand and use body language. You can take what you were born with and learn to signal more effectively, or you can belt out anything you feel like; it may or may not be on key. As a corollary, you can listen well and pick up the emotion behind the delivery, recognizing that the delivery is terrible.

Combine chemistry and judgment in both managing and understanding body language.

You Only Think You're Born Human

We always want to think about ourselves as some grand creature at the top of the food chain, but we aren't born that way. Children are not the humans we all become.

If you could magically turn a 2-year-old into an adult, with all of his current motor skills, language skills, and social skills, he could not support himself, and in some places would be institutionalized. Thankfully, nurturing and psychological development mean that most people turn into productive adults. Nurture plays a tremendous part in this development. Although the natural psychological development cycles will play out even in a vacuum, stimulus is required to create a functional adult from the canvas that is a child—so much so that feral children often never learn to speak. Turning again to the model of the bell curve, if feral children are the one extreme and precocious, highly groomed children at the other, most of us fall somewhere in the middle. Then our parents, extended social group, and education play a huge part in the mature humans we become.

From ultra-polished parents, we learn sublime signaling; from coarse parents, we learn coarse signaling. Then peer groups, teachers, bosses, and television each take their place in our nurture.

Spoken language, gesture, and unintentional messaging all have a part in this development, as does the native capacity of the child to grasp each of these pieces of nurture. This combination of nature and nurture create a wonderfully diverse population of human beings that has layers of difference that are not readily evident at first glance.

Although a feral child might have the same drives and desires as a nurtured child, the outcomes are dramatically different. The feral child is a socially starved human, and the nurtured human child, one that has been well fed. Born the same, only one becomes fully human with the skills of cultural gesturing and language that distinguish us from other primates.

Nurturing as a One-Way Street

Most parents start nurturing from first contact, or even in the womb, but are unaware of how much influence they exert on children during routine contact. A parent's natural response to pick up a crying baby teaches that baby that crying brings attention. The child learns something through every interaction in a chain of events. Of course the child's natural capacity influences what and how quickly he learns at the same time his temperament determines what he does with the stimulus. Although much of the nature of the child is likely hard-wired, expression of that temperament is conditioned by nurture. For example, an intensely curious child would be prone to stick her hand in a dog's mouth or pick up some strange, shiny object on the street. The curiosity is hard-wired; the awareness of safety issues is conditioning. Almost every change to a young child's behavior comes from directed stimulus created by the parent and continued until results are achieved. The child hears "Don't pick up things off the street" so many times that she finally alters her behavior.

Nurturing as a Two-Way Street

The way toddlers naturally signal normally endears them to their parents. The "nature" part that makes Junior sleep or sit like Dad makes Dad feel more comfortable in his paternity. It's just a product of physical form, but human beings tend to read emotional meanings into all kinds of things babies do. (When we do it with our house pets, it's called anthropomorphizing. When we do it with kids, it's called enthusiasm.) Other traits endear toddlers to all of us regardless of parentage. Oversized open eyes and heads and soft little faces show vulnerability and dependence on adults. This nature of humanity to love the large eyes and soft features is a response to the nature of our young, not their evolution to make us like them. (Ever wonder why the benevolent aliens in science-fiction movies have big heads and big eyes, but the evil ones bent on world domination look reptilian?) Watch upset toddlers in all but their most oppositional moods and  you can see some of the few instances of humans with wide open eyes that are crying. Large, open eyes are one of the first things children learn to control as they close their eyes shake their head and use the word they hear the most often every day: "No!"

Now think about wide-open, large eyes on an adult male. What impression do you get?

Masculinity?

Strength?

Confidence?

Sophistication?

Maturity?

Discipline?

How about: None of the above. Some signals just stop working after the age of 2.

The Emergence of Body Language Skills

In addition to some genetics-based signaling such as oversized eyes and soft features, certain movements naturally belong to the repertoire of expressions made by the human face. These basic signals are universally recognized and first codified through studies by Dr. Paul Ekman, the primary consultant on the television show *Lie to Me.* Although hard-wired and recognizable, their look depends on the facial shape and bone structure, which change the subtleties of these expressions. And although these signals are evident, often other, unintentional signaling is present at the same time, but it's not evident.

These first two layers of expressions set signaling patterns for humans. In getting used to his face, the toddler develops some basic survival tools. He starts to experiment with his own version of signaling in realizing he can do some odd things with his face—maybe purely unintentional in the beginning until a parent or sibling sees it and provides some form of stimulus to provoke it again. Based on input and his temperament as to whether he prefers to anger, enter-tain, tease, or appease his parent, this signaling can persist for any given amount of time, and maybe even into adulthood. (Probably every person reading this book has heard a version of this warning when parents finally get sick of an expression: "Do that again, and your face will stay like that!") In much the same way a child learns to control the wideness of his eyes, most male children realize through role models that men's noses do not wrinkle. So they rarely if ever voluntarily use that sig-nal in adulthood. The wrin-kled nose is clearly evident in unintentional signaling, as you will see in upcoming chapters.

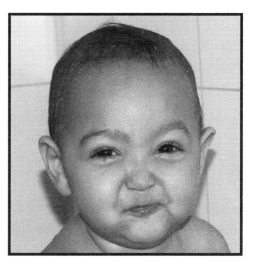

Lack of control is a hall-mark of children's body lan-guage—from flailing arms and big wide-open eyes, to loose jaws, slack faces, and sloppy posture. Parents typically chide their children to alter the cues of youth and move to a controlled, contained appearance. This physical control of self, as well as control over emotion, signifies intelligence and maturity in most cultures.

When Do We Learn to Fake It?

"When do people learn to do a fake smile?" The question came from a 14-year-old boy during a presentation on basic body language skills. We have awareness in infancy that doing certain things—grabbing and pushing, for example—gets results. But ba-bies have not yet developed enough awareness of self or situation to think through the causality: "If I shove that spoon away from my mouth, then she'll get the message I hate strained peas."

At a rodeo, I saw a boy of about 5 standing near me take one look at the bull charging into the ring and start imitating the bull; he became a bucking, running, stomping bull. A girl of 7 or 8 sitting on the fence in her shorts started swinging around the pole like a stripper. Kids at those young ages are reckless because they don't have a self-image to maintain. But not all kids have parents and teachers who allow freedom of expression. In some families and some cultures, self-awareness comes very early because adults "correct" children's movements and force them to use certain actions consciously. A 5-year-old girl in a beauty pageant knows perfectly well that a perfectly timed smile and a set of cutesy moves can help her please the judges.

The first models of deception start early. Parents teach children not to say exactly what they think with words or body language. "Do not stick your tongue out—that's not nice" and "Do not call Jimmy stupid" both teach politeness and limit natural expression. That means that children learn from an early age to fake specific messages. Other, more sophisticated lessons come later from parents, such as faking pleasure at seeing Aunt Molly until she is out of the house. Sophisticated deception requires self-awareness.

If you think back to when your self-image began to develop, that's probably when you learned to adopt body language to project a certain message, like a fake smile, and to think through the cause and effect relationships related to body language.

Your Filters Are Blinders

The influences of both nature and nurture create filters through which you perceive the sounds and movements of other people. If you're like most people, you are unaware of those influences, so you don't know what those filters block out or what comes through greatly intensified. You determine what people mean—the way the blind men determine what the elephant looks like.

Trading Places is a classic story of the power of consciously using body language to manipulate others to see what you want them to see—to use their filters so you get what you want. As the character Billy Ray Valentine, Eddie Murphy adopts the look of helplessness by pretending he has no legs or sight; he makes a good living as a beggar by preying on people's desire to save him from being society's victim. He does what all good con men do: He uses body language communication to exploit other people's beliefs and suppositions.

I do the same kind of thing to enhance communication with people at meetings as well as random encounters. So even though I know "when someone does x, it always means y" is generally a ridiculous assumption, I may do x specifically because that erroneous judgment is so popular. I use a common connotation of a gesture, the way someone saying "bad!" uses a common connotation of a word that used to mean—literally—"bad."

One of the skills you will learn here is to take the connotation away from your understanding of body language. You will see what it takes to create a non-verbal voice that can be understood by others.

Why We Do Things Over and Over

With Eddie Murphy and me, you have examples of intentional messaging. They are learned behaviors applied to elicit specific results. Eddie Murphy's intended outcome as the beggar is to arouse guilt and sympathy. Depending on the circumstance, I might do something like raise up on my toes to make you feel threatened or tap my feet to redirect your attention from something else I'm doing. As you learn to identify intentional body language, you will grow skillful at looking at what's behind it—what the real intent is.

More often than seeing deliberate messaging, you will see examples of how nature and nurture play out in unintentional messaging. You can take this unintentional body language at face value.

Someone who has a highly tuned sense of others' entitlements will leak emotions when she realizes she has stepped out of bounds and violated them. Even without saying a word, an aware observer would read "remorse" or "concern" in her body language. You read that and know you've seen the genuine message.

The opposite of someone like that would be a psychopath, a person who lacks empathy. He walks with abandon over other people as though they are property; they have no entitlements. In their book, *Snakes in Suits: When Psychopaths Go to Work*, Paul Babiak and Robert Hare examined people similar to that in business, partly to help the rest of us spot the signs of these destructive personalities. Any remorse or concern you would see coming from a person such as that reflects a deliberate attempt to manipulate, or remorse at being caught.

Whether the messages are delivered intentionally or unintentionally, the behaviors will be repeated as long as they are rewarded. That is why we do things over and over. If you find that ultra-masculine or ultra-feminine behavior causes other people to be deferential to you during meetings, you will turn it on when you want a good dose of deference.

Take another look at the twisted face of the toddler earlier in this chapter. The photographer either got very lucky in capturing that face, or someone such as the child's mother knew exactly how to provoke that expression. I'd bet on the latter, with her saying "Make the funny face for Mommy!" and then giving him a hug when he does it.

Normal or Abnormal?

Years ago, I took a very proper British woman to a Thai restaurant and warned her not to order something hot because she'd had no exposure to Thai food. Ignoring me, she ordered a dish ranked 3 on a scale of 1 to 5, with 5 being the maximum. They brought her food. She put a spoonful in her mouth, stood up, and screamed profanities at the wait staff.

Whether a person tones down or amplifies normal behavior, that deviation indicates something key about intent. The more desperate the need to communicate a message becomes, the more the expression will deviate from an individual's baseline.

Your baseline body language is what is normal for you—that is, the natural surfacing of all of those nature and nurture influences in the way you sound and move. At 5 years old, you may have picked up quirky gestures, such as winking when you say yes or shifting your hips when you say no. Other people often read meaning into them because they don't do those things. But they are part of your baseline—part of your "normal."

As a matter of course in reading body language, you will make note of the difference between normal and abnormal for the person you are trying to read.

Often, I'm asked to analyze the body language of celebrities after they've done something scandalous. I get questions such as "Can you tell if she's lying?" and "Was he upset, or was it just an act?" Depending on the context, sometimes I can jump into an analysis such as that and give a reading because I see certain universal signs or body language that I know is glitchy for the person. Generally, however, I want to view footage of the person under more normal circumstances than the current trauma so I can get a baseline. With a baseline, I'm in a strong position to detect emotions and intentions; I can get a lot deeper into the person's psyche.

Here's what you can miss without a baseline: When nighttime talk show host David Letterman made a crude joke about former Alaska Governor Sarah Palin's daughter, he incurred the wrath of lots more people than Governor Palin. Responding to pressure to apologize, he spent about four minutes of his monologue one night on damage control. Even though she accepted his apology, the consensus in the media was that it did not have a ring of sincerity. Some criticized him for the way he moved his hands and his eyes and the tone of his voice—obviously insincere, they thought.

In a situation with someone who has delivered monologue after monologue the same way year after year, to come across as sincere would require a deviation from the norm. So David Letterman could not come across as sincere without a change from his usual presentation style. He didn't, and popular opinion declared him insincere. Repetition leaves a mark and crinkles the canvas. Letterman's body language of years of the same delivery just does not work for an apology. He needed to go against the marks and crinkles.

Without knowledge of the influences on another person's expression, the human tendency is to see what you want to see and to rely on your filters as you interpret someone else's body language. You probably don't issue a sincere apology to someone by sitting behind a desk, clasping your hands, and occasionally inserting a laugh line. Therefore when you see David Letterman do that, you assume he isn't sincere either.

The most significant message of this chapter is that the many influences on us make "normal" a little different for all of us. If we are ever to read each other's body language accurately, we have to spot the difference between normal and abnormal for each and every person.

I Am Normal AND You Are Normal

How do you polish your "non-verbal voice"? It starts with awareness. Just as an Alabama accent or a Brooklyn accent is not wrong, neither is any given way of non-verbal communication. The key to relating is identical to speaking with someone who uses a different variation of English. You have to take conscious steps to ensure that your choice of words, or signals in this case, conveys the meaning you intend. Having basic meaning as well as nuances be understood requires paying attention. If you go into the conversation with bravado and nonchalance, assuming the person understands, you could have a rude awakening when you realize she missed your point, or even worse, was offended. During your conversation each of the five nurtured factors in addition to your natural factors come into play, so keep them in mind: self-awareness, sophistication, situational awareness, a sense of others' entitlement and what is proper, and personal style, or grooming.

Generations of speech patterns leave behind a well-accepted way of communicating that often includes the verbal equivalent of gestures. These include words whose original meaning has long since left our understanding, but usage keeps them alive. Phrases such as *whole nine yards* and giving someone the *third degree* are in common usage and with a shared understanding. People repeat them routinely without even knowing the original meanings: all the bullets in the chain on a fighter aircraft in World War II, and the grilling of a Masonic candidate for the third degree that would make him more than an apprentice, respectively. As you think about body language such as gesture and intentional signaling, keep these thoughts in mind. Much of what anyone does is habit. Normal is what he normally does. Normal is how he behaves when not responding to stimulus. That is his baseline. Although it might be very different from yours, just like his accent, it is his normal.

Chapter 2

What Is Universal?

W hat do crossed arms mean? Did the people in these photos think through the process of crossing their arms to convey a particular meaning, or did they adopt this position instinctively? And are they conveying the same meaning?

Answer these questions based on what you know right now, and then later in the book, when we build to a discussion of holistic interpretation of body language, compare you, new answers to the original ones.

Universal and Involuntary

Human beings do not plan everything we do with our faces and bodies. Sometimes our genes run the machine.

To raise your skills in reading and using body language, you need a solid grasp of what people do that is universal and involuntary. I don't mean that we execute the moves in precisely the same way; to some extent, our muscle and skeletal structures dictate how we move. But we can easily see commonalities in the way people express certain emotions and attempt to convey some basic messages. In addition, all humans share some types of movements regardless of culture, gender, or language.

A great deal of why we understand the moves, as different as they may look, is because of the elements of focus and engagement.

Where a person directs her attention is the simple definition of *focus*. Someone sitting in a room glancing casually across it at a group of people without really concentrating on an object or person might easily be consumed by things other than those in the room. This means that her eyes might drift and seem to pay attention to you, but her mind is involved somewhere else.

Humans can divide attention only so far, so a person might hang up the phone and center on you with his eyes with no genuine sense of interaction with you. His focus is internal, but his energy is directed toward thoughts and feelings sparked by the phone call. He might even gesture as though he is in conversation with you, making his points with his head, hands, face, and eyes. The man in this photo is using his hand to drive home a point. Anyone in the room can clearly understand he is punctuating a thought. Only problem is, no one else is in the room. He is on a conference call and alone, driving his point nonetheless. This is normal behavior—not  just for him, but for most of us. After he hangs up the phone and starts to pay attention to you, he is now truly focused on you. That focus alone does not indicate engagement.

Think of engagement as contact. Not simply directing his attention to you but tying all of that energy through a given channel to make contact. Eye contact is not always a part of engagement, although it usually is the first part of the interaction. A person looking away can still be engaged with you, just as someone making

eye contact can have no intent to communicate with you. In successful flirting, for example, one person might break eye contact and look at the other with a passing glance. The result is a "come here" kind of alluring contact. There is no eye lock like the look of an obsessed stalker; the attraction is that the person is issuing an invitation. How eyes move as part of conversation is covered more in future chapters, but be aware that eye contact even in American culture is sporadic and natural, and not locked. Most of us are instinctively uncomfortable when someone stares without an attempt to communicate.

A person can even turn her entire torso away from you as she sits and spins a chair and yet clearly remain engaged with you. In fact, often torso, head, and eye signaling will break, yet the engagement is clear and unbroken.

Focus, Engagement, and Signaling

The amount of focus and engagement between two people affects their ability to signal with body language. The interplay of intentional and unintentional signaling adds a level of complexity. Grasping these factors is therefore a foundation of reading body language. If a person is focused on you but not engaged, he may be telegraphing messages about his internal thoughts to the outside world more than conversing with you. Or he may be focused and engaged, but trying to signal the thoughts he wants to share only with you. There is a good chance those thoughts will come out as unintentional signaling.

Classes of Gesture

Body language includes "gestures" that are almost universal. Things like shaking the head left to right to signify "no" has meaning in large portions of the world. Desmond Morris in *The Naked Ape* postulated it was the most universal gesture because it was derived from a baby turning his head away from the nipple. He also asserted that a nod for "yes" was a motion for more milk.

These symbols are not truly universal, though. The dividing line appears to happen somewhere around the former Ottoman Empire. Arabs and Greeks use a quick rise of the head, almost as if throwing the head back, to indicate no. In the Middle East, it is often accompanied by a "tisk" sound made by drawing the tongue down from the roof of the mouth. Arabs and Greeks also typically use a sudden lowering of the head with a tilt to affirm something. That is easily recognizable by the Western world, though it is not a common signal. The nodding and shaking we use appears to be easy enough for Middle Eastern people to understand as well. As you move to the Indian subcontinent, movement of the head to message becomes much more subtle and mysterious to non-natives.

Other symbols can be almost universal because they are beckoning or expelling moves. It is hard to imagine that any body movement involving thrusting the open facing palm of the hand towards you is a welcoming move. Or to imagine that any extending of hands or fingers followed by a retracting toward your body is other than a beckoning one.

The style of the beckoning move might differ from one continent to the next, but at its root the basic movement is the same in

Europe, Africa, Asia, and North America. For example, take a look at this photo of Kofi suggesting "come here" in a gesture common

to his culture. Imagine his fingers extended and then retracted back to his palm. This same gesture is used in Korea. This gesture does not differ fundamentally from the North American version, except the palm is down. In both Korean and Ghana culture, placing the palm up is used to summon animals or as a derogatory to other people.

Although you would miss that nuance, the basic message is intact. And if you're honestly trying to understand each other, you would figure it out without any sense of disrespect. Assuming you were both attempting to communicate, he would simply turn his or your palm down to illustrate your mistake and you would have a common message.

Most expelling body language is meant to force someone away. Greeks use a palm and stiffened fingers shoved forward at you. In some cultures, people spit on the ground. These types of explosive gestures are not usually beckoning, and that fact is universally easy to see.

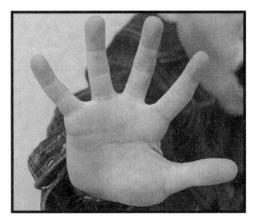

Universal Facial Expressions

Humans have evolved certain facial expressions that are so universal that all but the least perceptive individuals can recognize them. I hope your reaction to seeing a lot of these photos is "A-ha! I knew that." But as you look at multiple photos of the same expression side by side, I also hope you see more. Each universal expression has degrees, and the differences resulting from bone structure, skin tone, and other physical characteristics combine with slightly different mental states to cause variations.

The reason certain expressions fall into the category of "universal" is grounded in research with diverse populations. Most notably, multiple studies conducted by Paul Ekman of the Human Interaction Laboratory at the University of California's School of Medicine affirm the observation that certain facial expressions are universal to all humans. In all of my years of having to read people quickly to assess their emotional state, I would agree with the basic list of six he covers in "Facial Expression and Emotion: An Old Controversy and New Findings" (*The Royal Society,* 1992): disgust, sadness, fear, anger, surprise, and enjoyment (or happiness). To those I would add contempt, pride, uncertainty, and embarrassment, versions of which did make it into Ekman's later lists. People try to mask them, but they still come out, and, as humans, we have a natural ability of humans to interpret that base body language.

What emotion are all of these faces conveying to you?

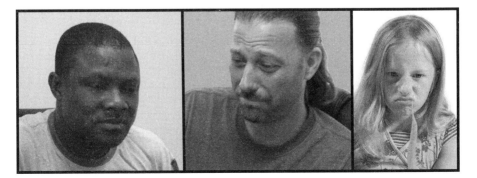

Each in his own way is displaying disgust. The man on the left, a recent immigrant to the United States from Ghana, tends to use constrained body language. Look at the lack of lines on his face and contrast that with the picture of Brian, who is just about five years older. Whether the constrained body language is a personal choice or cultural is a tough call by looking at one person. Biology and bone structure often play as big a part as culture. Brian's expression of disgust in looking at the same photo as the man on his left shows why he has earned the lines on his face. Interestingly, even in this photo capturing his disgust, you can also see the lines around his mouth commonly called laugh lines. From this one photo then, you can see how the phrase "by 40, you've earned the face you have" comes true with Brian, who is 39. As for the girl, she's responding with a display of disgust that would apply equally to a plate of broccoli and the sight of road kill. And if she keeps up that level of reaction, her face will be a readable record of her emotions by the time she is Brian's age. Among the most receptive of muscles to this patterning is the brow muscle, referred to as the "grief muscle" by the French. I jokingly refer to it as the Botox muscle because it is the primary target of that drug.

Bodies adapt to what we do. A long-distance runner who decides to take up weight training and become a competitive bodybuilder has to make adjustments in the way muscles are used—to recondition them the way you would tune a piano. When the wires become accustomed to holding one shape, the piano tuner has a big job: He has to come back repeatedly to condition the wires to stay in tune. The same thing happens with your face. Muscle memory kicks in and dictates how you use it, and shows all the world how you have used it in the past.

Of all the facial expressions listed—disgust, sadness, fear, anger, surprise, happiness, contempt, and pride—what do you see here?

All three have a clear, external focus, raised chin, and set mouth that suggests pride.

A look of pride can be associated with both positive and negative situations, but the emotion is the same. When a police officer confronts a gang member in front of his buddies, the gang member will stand indignantly, raise his head, and flash pride. It may just be the pride of "I got your attention." But in the photo on the right, the kid is showing pride after doing something his dad is proud of. Both are pride rooted in accomplishment and acknowledgment.

The reason this little guy is crying seems clear—and he is signaling a single emotion with his whole body. Well-meaning parents have offered him the opportunity to try horseback riding. His face vividly demonstrates unbridled fear of the kind we rarely see in adults. His engagement is with his trusted allies—his parents—and not with the big, hairy beast. In an expression of fear, the muscle between the brows engages, bringing the brow to a peak. The lower face may stay flat and uninvolved, or fully involved in terror as the person shouts or cries in an outburst.

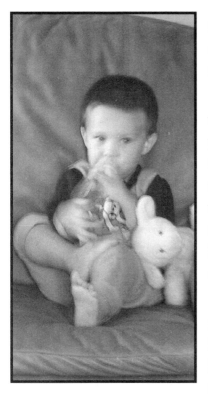

This photo captures the baseline for the same child. Hours before meeting the horse, he was fully relaxed with no brow involvement.

Even someone who knows you well and feels comfortable with you will occasionally show some of the same signs of uncertainty that a stranger, or someone unfamiliar with your culture, will show. You can surprise her with a request or ask for her opinion on a topic that causes anxiety, for example.

Despite Brian's familiarity with me, when I asked him to participate in a photo session for this book, he had no idea what I would ask him to do. He had a look of uncertainty. While I explained the process to him, I could see that he was interpreting what I was saying, trying to organize the information so he would be ready to give me what I wanted. Uncertainty can be a negative or a positive emotion. In Brian's case, it was weighted to the positive, the way the uncertainty associated with a first date or trip to Disneyland might be positive. Jodi's uncertainty takes a bit of middle-of-the-road approach.

She shows a characteristic polite smile with a containment of head movement and attention to the details I am giving her. Her uncertainty about the request is evident until I have clarified how I will use the photographs.

Contrast their expressions with the uncertainty of Kofi, unfamiliar with both me and the American culture. Immediately after coming into the room, he sat down in a chair behind a table, gripped the arms of the chair, shuffled his feet, and gave me this look of uncertainty.

In the upcoming section (Common Movements), you will see the significance of where he chose to sit and how he handled his body in this initial encounter. His whole body, not just his face, conveyed uncertainty. There is rigidness and unnatural movement to the torso and neck in uncertainty that prevents natural flow, and it shows to a different degree based on the level of uncertainty of the person.

With some emotions, you don't even need the whole face. The eyes say it all. It is all part of why for generations we've been quoting the proverb "the eyes are the windows to the soul."

Common Movements

We have talked about gesture as intentional, negotiated, silent words. Additionally there are four big categories of body language that all humans have in common: barriers, adaptors, regulators, and illustrators. Depending on your gender, physical make-up, and the context, they can look very different from person to person. At the same time, they always play the same role in your communication.

BARRIERS

Using barriers is the most natural thing we do to claim more ground and to increase the amount of space around us. Whether the barrier is an object (a desk, a computer, a plate of food), part of our body (arms, shoulder), or a movement (turn to the side), it helps us establish boundaries as clearly as a fence around a yard. Barriers also provide a sense of protection. When you put a purse or computer bag between you and another person, turn your side to someone in a crowd, or sit on the opposite side of a table, you have some sense of being less vulnerable. People at cocktail parties hold their drinks and hors d'oeuvres plate directly in front of them as they talk with strangers. When they loosen up with a second drink and/or get to know the other person a little better, they then move those barriers to the side. This creates a sense of shared space and suggests the need for "protection" no longer exists.

In combat, there are two ways of using barriers: cover and concealment. Cover means you can't hit me with a bullet. Concealment means you can't see me. A young soldier who confuses the two is not a successful soldier. Many of the barriers we use on a day-to-day basis are concealment, not cover. We hide behind something flimsy, even though it makes us feel safe.

In some cases a barrier is cover, however. Sitting behind a desk allows you to hide activity from the chest down. Depending on your height, standing behind a podium can be part of an effort to create a head-to-toe cover and concealment operation: A short person wearing glasses with a microphone positioned in front of the face and a podium obscuring the body from the neck down could be so barriered you wouldn't even know the speaker's gender. This kind of whole-body barriering is less than typical and demands a staged setting. Most barriering is a target of opportunity and as a result it is improvised.

One of the most mistaken barriers in American culture is crossed arms. In the series of four photos you looked at earlier, that gesture is likely the first thing you see about each of the people, which is a natural human response to pattern-seeking. There is other, whole-body messaging occurring in each of these posed photographs, covered later, that conveys the real message. Although the folded arms can mean a person needs more space, it can also mean she feels physically comfortable standing this way due to physiology. To assert more would be disregarding what is normal for the individual.

Remember the five factors when you are considering any movement in a vacuum. This reminder fully applies to arm-crossing. Humans are the premier tool-users on earth, and we were born with a set of tools that makes that possible: our hands. When we become self-aware, one of the first things we are aware of is how they look. As we develop more situational awareness and become more sophisticated, we try to find things to do with our hands. A person might decide to fold his arms because he can't think of anything else to do with his hands, and that becomes so ingrained that, even when he feels comfortable, it is a default setting. Or, it could be a real barrier to feel safer.

Why could all of these sets of crossed arms actually be barriers? You might want to use the posture because you need space to think, you've concluded that the person you're talking to is an idiot and you want to put separation between the two of you, or you feel mildly threatened.

From mildly threatened to profoundly threatened, men commonly barrier their genitals by crossing their hands in front of them. My name for it is protecting the precious. Watch men unaccustomed to public speaking. Even though they may be behind a podium, you will see their hands down in a fig-leaf position—a double barrier. Men typically cover their genitals when they are under any kind of stress. Sophistication, self-awareness, grooming, and situational awareness help to remove this most primal of signals.

Women, if you find this amusing, not so fast. You have your own version of protecting the precious that I refer to as "egg protecting." When women feel the need to barrier and feel more control over environment you simply cross your arm(s) over your abdomen. Just comfortable you say? That's the same thing a man would say about reverting to the fig leaf. In the case of this young lady, I pointed out that she was fidgeting with her hair when she spoke with me and she immediately crossed her abdomen. As much push-back as I get from women about my label for it, this is a common barrier.

In a work environment, people have myriad ways to keep others at a distance in their offices and cubicles. They stack papers on the desk so you have to look around or over them to make eye contact with the office occupant. They put things at the edge of the cube to "decorate," with the effect being that your attention is more on the cartoons on the periphery of the cube than on the center of it where they "live." Both types of measures help establish a person's space; in a crowded office, especially where people sit in cube after cube, that kind of barriering provides a measure of sanity.

Barriers are rarely intentional messaging, but they are deliberate sometimes. A mobile barrier—that is, something you carry with you—may become something a person consciously makes part of her daily repertoire. A purse of any size can serve as a barrier for a woman in public place, and for many women it's recognized as such. They have the concept reinforced by a mother or other mentor that, when they are walking with a friend or boyfriend, they should switch the side the shoulder bag is on to the outside. Some mobile barriers, like an amulet or religious medallion, can actually be invisible to the outside world and yet serve as protection for the wearer. One of the most significant barriers we see in Western society is a wedding ring. It can clearly be used to defend a woman's space and delineate a perimeter. If the barrier seems to be invisible to others, she might even reinforce the barrier by rubbing it with a thumb or adjusting it with the opposite hand to call attention to the importance of the barrier.

ADAPTORS

If using a barrier helps you establish private space, then using an adaptor gives you the opportunity to gain or regain control over that space. Adaptors may be used in conjunction with or separate from barriers. When you notice someone twirling her hair or stroking her neck as the young woman from the egg-protector photos was doing, this is an attempt to make herself more comfortable. All people have some version of an adaptor, whether they do it constantly or only under high stress. Most people are unaware of their adaptors because they are focused on the cause of the adaptor at the time they are using it. This is why a person focused but not engaged is sending unintentional messaging, particularly about insecurity levels.

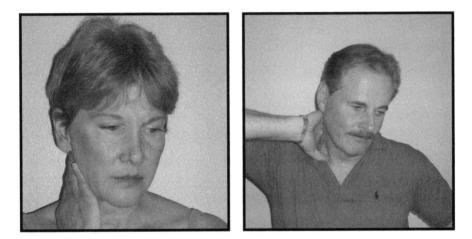

Adaptors make you feel more comfortable. They are the rubbing, petting, hair-twirling family of gestures that may be obvious or subtle. Sometimes, they take on the form of a ritual, which you often see at sports events: the batter rubbing his legs before grabbing the bat, the golfer stroking the brim of his visor before he tees off, the tennis player scratching the side of her racket with a fingernail. Gestures such as these enable you to feel more energetically focused and in control. Many times, adaptors are idiosyncratic, and they tend to differ by gender.

Women rely on gentle stroking gestures more than men; men often make their adaptors vigorous, and would more likely rub than pet.

There is no end to the list of actions that can become adaptors: pacing, scratching, twisting, clicking, sucking on teeth. If you can imagine the action, then it can become a stress adaptor, depending on the context. People will do almost anything to release nervous energy.

Adaptors are often accompanied by other bits of body language. Both of these photos show internal focus and inner voice concentration, which means the cause of their adaptors is internal. Internal in this case means that, whether the issue started externally or not, the issue has moved to one of internal conversation for resolution; even without training, it's easy to see the object of their obsession is internal. The photo of the male shows a common adaptor for high stress, especially around working through an issue.

Kofi uses both an adaptor and a barrier as he begins his interview with me. He grips the arms of the chair (adaptor), which he has pulled toward the table (barrier). And he can reinforce that barrier easily by not even making eye contact.

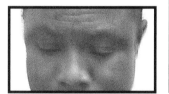

Intensity can also indicate the level of stress or stimulus involved. Knowing a person's baseline enables you to determine intensity. Compare this baseline photo for Kofi, who normally shows very little animation, with other photos of him, such as the one of him in this section.

Idiosyncratic behavior can mean that a person in an obsessive manner can stroke, pet, twist, twirl, or rub himself constantly without meaning, while the slightest tweak from another person can indicate great discomfort. Consider the five factors when you are reviewing adaptors, because they can all contribute to what becomes idiosyncratic behavior.

Both men and women can have varying degrees of adaptors. Adapting is not typically a conscious endeavor but, when people are aware you can read them, they are more likely to be cautious. Notice Jodi's right hand. She is adapting by placing fingertip to thumb as if pinching. This is a relatively common and sophisticated way to channel energy that would find its way through feet, hands, fingers, and toes tapping and sending out the code of uncertainty and discomfort.

Baseline is everything; look for normal and then find deviations. Just remember that adaptors are unintentional, but some people are sophisticated enough to be able to use something that appears to be an adaptor with intention. If you want to convey a subliminal message that you are nervous and out of control, that could be a way to do it.

Regulators

Regulators control another person's speech. Seasoned comedians use regulators well to tell their audiences when to laugh. Raising a hand or a pen in a stop-sign manner during a meeting is a regulator, sometimes used subtly and unintentionally, that suggests "I've heard enough from you; now it's my turn to talk."

A regulator is usually intentional and can take any form that can be recognized by the intended audience. Teachers and parents generally develop looks—with eyebrows and the tilt of a head—that signal it's time to talk or time to shut up. Other gestures used as regulators might be pointing the index finger laterally across the body and rolling it like a wheel to indicate hurry or creating a T with both hands to signify time out. For these silent words to work, each party must understand them.

Connotations may jump out at the subject of a regulator, meaning that the person receiving the signal might construe that your attempt to control the conversation is offensive, overbearing, feigned interest, or a number of other emotionally charged motivations. If the person takes offense, for example, she might have some strong body language in response to the regulator.

More than any other group of signals this one is closely tied to the sense of others' entitlements and can easily be misconstrued. Consider a regulator to be the silent-voice equivalent of the imperative form of the verb. You most likely wouldn't shout "Stop!" or "Shut up!" or "Get on with it!" to a coworker, so when your body language does it, don't be surprised if you provoke a negative response.

On occasion, unintentional signaling can result from repeated use of regulators and lack of focus. A mother who is also a businesswoman, for example, might easily find herself distracted during a meeting. She allows her brain to telegraph its thoughts about the boss's statement with a regulator she commonly uses to control her children. Other unintentional signaling can occur when a person uses an adaptor that is clearly understood to mean "enough." Although not an intentional regulator, something like rubbing the grief muscle at the brow with the eyes closed and head tilted will surely have the same effect.

ILLUSTRATORS

Illustrators punctuate your statements. I often say it is your brain punctuating thoughts. Often, your arms do the work—pointing in a particular direction, forearm moving like an orchestra conductor's baton—but your head, shoulders, or even your whole body can get involved. A person can use any part of his body to make a point, from Adolph Hitler whipping his audience with his rhetoric to former President Bill Clinton using a symbolic baton to drive home his denial of having an affair with Monica Lewinsky. We like to see what someone means, and illustrators support that. When Robin Williams tells funny stories, everything, including his eyes, illustrates the punch lines.

If the photo here looks vaguely familiar, that's because you saw the entire picture in the Introduction, where I explained that the person in the photo, Kofi, is from Ghana and this gesture referred to food, as in "let's eat." Focusing only on his arm, you could conclude that it's simply an illustrator.

By punctuating the meanings of words and concepts, illustrators help us to get our points across. Looking at this photo, you can readily understand that Kim is differentiating one concept from the other in a discussion with the photographer. The imagery of her illustrators is so in sync

with her words that you do not need to know what she is saying to understand that the conversation included "On one hand, they...."

Illustrators are most often intentional signaling but can leak unintentional signaling as well, especially when a person tries to contain body language. The best indicator that this is occurring is that the illustrator does not make the same point as the speaker's words. CSPAN's coverage of congressional hearings provides plenty of examples as politicians gesticulate—probably so they won't look like statues in front of the cameras—but their movements and words have nearly nothing to do with one another. The incongruity might also suggest a lie. The man who uses his hands to indicate the fish was "this big," but has his hands so far away from his body that he can barely see them, might be sending a message that even he doesn't believe his story and prefers not to see the lie.

Orchestration

You will often see a couple of the big four movements combined, and you may even see all four in play at once. Someone giving a speech, for example, may be curling his toes (adaptor) while standing behind a podium (barrier), using his hands to punctuate a point (illustrator), and pausing to allow the audience to applaud (regulator). In this next photo, you see how Brian's right hand illustrates a point while his left hand remains rooted on a barrier.

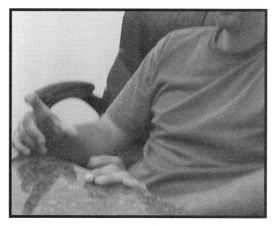

Take another look at the photo of Kofi using his eyes as a barrier. Here is the rest of it, capturing what I would call a dynamic adaptor. After being very constrained throughout the session, he finally made a large move; he seemed to think there was a bug on him. He over-reacted, which is a typical response for someone who has a need to express himself, but doesn't feel he can do so normally. So this wasn't just about the scratching; it was about adapting to the situation.

How the Big Four Serve

Barriers, adaptors, regulators, and illustrators are like verbs, prepositions, nouns, and articles. Each plays a part in the sentence that is body language. Any of the elements alone is incomplete in much the same way using an individual word is most often not a complete thought. The exception is using a regulator in a commanding way.

Most often, each of the four parts of non-verbal speech will tie together to create good, effective sentences to people who read body language holistically. To anyone in that group, body language is as sublime and coherent a form of communication as spoken language can be. Prior to undertaking this study of how to read and use body language, on some level you have perceived pieces of it, but it probably means that the real message someone was sending escaped you. By fine-tuning this signaling and receiving, you can over-pronounce other non-verbal messages that others do not get the first time, and negotiate meaning to add new words and phrases to your non-verbal voice. First, however, you have to take into account all of the elements that impact how the person receives your message and transmits her own.

Chapter 3

Cultural Standards

Two key concepts come into play in a discussion of cultural differences in body language. One is projection: When you assume that a particular gesture means something because it means something in your culture, you are no longer in a position to understand the real message. This is a continuation of the Chapter 1 discussion of filters influenced by nature and nurture and the primary focus of this chapter. First, consider the other concept: limits of expression imposed by the brain and body.

Whatever It Is, You've Seen It Before

The media has enlightened the whole world to gestures by pop culture icons. Gestures that used to be seen only on the streets of Los Angeles or during an American football game are now being used by people half a world away who have never been to the United States. As I define a gesture, it is a movement that has been agreed upon and is understood by all parties involved.

You may give the media credit for the shared understanding that turns some actions into a gesture, but there is something more basic at work that causes many more gestures to be ubiquitous.

Humans have a finite number of brain patterns. They are limited enough by physiology that we can understand many gestures of our ape ancestors, and the apes can understand us. We may think we're brilliant in coming up with secret codes, but there is a reason why code-breakers can decipher anything other humans come up with: There are only so many ways the brain works. You think you're the first one to come up with a particular idea? Think again.

To prove the point, which of these would you say reflects truly fresh thinking:

a) The Secret, popularized by the book of the same name by Rhonda Byrne, is the "Law of Attraction"—that is, a magnetic effect your feelings put in motion. Positive begets positive; negative begets negative.

b) Eckhart Tolle suggests that living in the "now" is the path to happiness and enlightenment.

Regarding choice a, one of the many sources discussing the manifestation of wealth and happiness is the Kabbalah, a set of teachings on the mystical aspects of Judaism. It's about 1,000 years old.

Regarding choice b, Buddha would be proud.

When you think of Hitler and the Nazis, what is the first gesture you associate with them? Chances are it's the straight-armed salute that accompanied "Heil, Hitler!" If you think this was a Nazi invention, you wouldn't be alone, but you probably would be surprised to learn that it was in common use in the United States prior to World War II as a salute to the American flag. Called the Bellamy salute, it was introduced to the United States as part of a

Columbus Day Celebration on October 12, 1892, by Francis Bellamy of Rome, New York. The author of the Pledge of Allegiance, Bellamy intended it to be used during the Pledge of Allegiance. But before Bellamy co-opted it, the gesture was known as the Roman Salute. In the 1920s, Italian Fascists renewed use of it in support of their claims to rebuilding the Roman Empire. The Nazis quickly hijacked this imagery and made it their own. The United States officially replaced the Bellamy Salute in June 1942, with the adoption of the Flag Code by Congress. This was not before great confusion on the part of many Americans and great fervor around Nazi-hunting during World War II.

This is not to suggest that humans lack diversity of thought and creativity associated with each person's uniqueness. It is to say that collectively we have likely considered nearly every topic imaginable in the past. Some of it was not provable scientifically when first proposed, or may have surfaced in a primitive way, but someone thought of it because human thought is finite. Add to that the limited range of motions humans have and the predefined expression already covered, and you quickly realize that culture is more about standards of acceptance and curtailing or grooming behaviors than it is about establishing new ones. In that way, this set of social mores we call culture is like a super-parental effect governing all who participate.

Culture or Sub-Culture: Identifying Your Own Cultural Standards

Cultures vary in size from multinational down to local tribe. Typically, a culture that is a component of a larger group can be considered a sub-culture, just as vegans are a sub-culture of vegetarians. Although the United States has on overarching culture that reflects our style of democracy, economic system, freedom of the press, and so on, multiple sub-cultures thrive in American society.

In general, parents try to get their kids to behave by asking them to modify their body language. What they're saying is, really, "Don't leak your true feelings." They are trying to be politically and culturally sensitive so that their kids do not go through life hurting people's feelings; it is part of making their children functional adults. Even though it's in the name of good manners, without even knowing what they're doing, these parents are instilling a protective habit into their kids. It does not serve us well to go around letting our body language blurt out what we're thinking and feeling. How each sub-culture curtails the natural behavior of its youngest members varies from unit to unit. Each takes the intent of making the younger members more productive and higher-functioning members of the group, and applies it a little differently.

The instruction can seem excessive, though, as Maryann experienced early in her education.

The teaching order of nuns in her school—many, if not all of them—felt strongly that excessive gesturing was a sign of insanity, or at least a lack of class. The challenge some of them used was to describe a spiral staircase without using your hands. The exercise gave students practice in using language descriptively without rotating hands and arms. The irony is that they forced many of those kids into adaptive behavior that involved a whole different set of movements. Those inclined to use illustrators freely because of their family's habits and culture had to suppress that tendency to please the good Sisters. As they complied and did the prescribed exercise, I wonder how many of them were wiggling their toes, shuffling their feet, squinting their eyes, and swallowing more than normal? All of these are adaptors.

What the nuns who enforced the code of restraint didn't realize is that it's normal for people to communicate through more than one channel. The ability to talk with your hands is an important type of physical communication; the restraint of such a natural means of communication creates stress. Stress finds its way to the surface through adaptors. These children were simply communicating in a manner the good Sisters did not understand in the way that you do now.

When the young men and women who had practiced this controlled behavior for years decided to deviate, it was very likely because they felt emotionally charged about something. They reverted to what came naturally, maybe even overcompensating.

The opposite of the Sisters' cultural training occurs where "redneck" behavior is encouraged. Unrestrained, honest expressions of emotions are the hallmark of American "rednecks," who have counterparts in cultures around the globe. Although within this "redneck" culture there are still harsh codes of behavior and what is acceptable, they are the people who abstain from the proper social behavior of mainstream society because it's meaningless to them— whether by choice or lack of understanding.

There are social advantages and disadvantages to behaving this way. The advantage is that people who behave this way tend to be less restrained, and communicate through gesture and illustrator more freely, resulting in less need to use adaptors. Men without adaptors come across as alpha males; they seem exceedingly sure of themselves, and that elicits deferential behavior from men who are not. The disadvantage is that this unrestrained kind of expression is unsophisticated—that is, completely lacking polish. The range of environments where it's appropriate is extremely limited. Of course, the four factors play heavily into this, and the keenly self-aware "redneck" will feel awkward if he has situational awareness as well, because he will realize his total lack of sophistication places him at a disadvantage and he will then start to use adaptors.

Sophisticated people (using the traditional meaning)—the kind the nuns in Maryann's school tried to cultivate—suppress natural body language and substitute mannerisms and gestures of other sophisticated people. Because there is a certain degree of artificiality in the expressions, unsophisticated folks may not know what they mean. This precise kind of misinterpretation lies at the heart of many moments in Shakespeare's comedies as well as TV sitcoms. In *Frasier*, the two psychiatrist brothers, Niles and Frasier Crane, frequently left their ex-cop father in the dark about what they meant with their gestures and shifts in the pitch of their voices. But put a "redneck" in a room full of pretentious people, and everyone there will know what he's trying to communicate simply because he is relying on rudimentary signaling that every child understands and was forced to leave behind as he matured.

In terms of breaking away from what we've been trained to do, a lot of us struggle with that fact that we don't know how to deviate so that our new actions make sense to us or anyone else. Culture impacts body language by pairing options to create meanings. The examples we have discussed are examples in American culture. Now let's take a look at a few things that have meaning in other cultures to better define baselines for the people who belong to them.

How universal are these seemingly natural and significant hand signals?

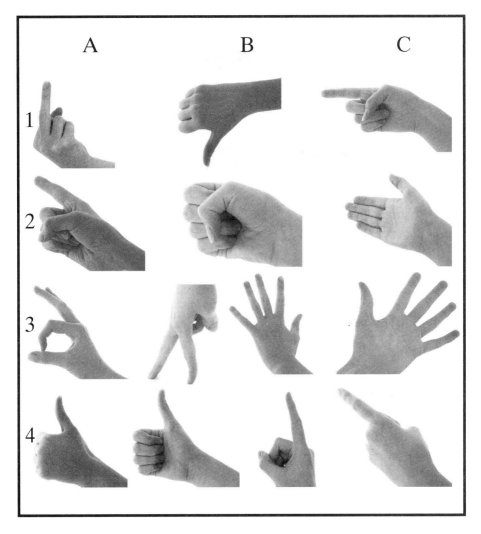

Based on Kofi's understanding, the middle finger (A1) gets the message across partly due to the ubiquitous influence of American culture. The mimicry messages, like walking fingers in B3, still get the point across as well. The thumbs-down in B1 not so much.

As for okay in A3, Kofi says this reminds him of a gesture he knew from him native land, which has a sexual message.

Pushing the hand forward, as in C3, is a clear affront in Greece where it is called a "moutza." Greeks use this as a gesture of insult and it may be paired with words that mean things like "take this." They also build on this with an even more offensive gesture by using both hands, and then hitting the palm of one hand against the back of the other toward the 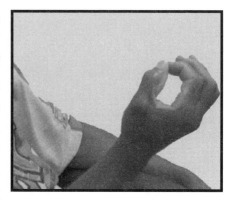 person being insulted. The closer someone does it to another person's face, the meaner it is. Interestingly, because the extension of a hand like this could mean nothing more than the answer to the question "How many children do you have?" with the answer being "five," when Greeks want to say "five," they face their palm inward, so that the person who asked the question sees the back of their hand.

The thumbs-up seen in A4 would be considered rude in most Middle Eastern countries due to the use of the left hand, which is reserved for hygiene, rather than contact with other people or eating. More importantly, the gesture throughout many of those countries has the meaning "up yours." Although contact with Americans has tempered meaning of the gesture, strong aversion to the left hand in the Gulf States means that even soldiers must pay attention to signaling out of concerns for offending someone.

Obviously, other cultures have used these same signals to mean different things, and, now that human beings have more exchanges on a global level than in previous centuries, the differences can make or break the quality of a first contact. In short, seemingly innocuous hand signaling and body language that people in one culture take for granted can easily assume a different meaning in another culture.

Most Americans' understanding of these symbols and signals has come from common usage across Northern Europe carried across the Atlantic. After World War II, a lot of European words and gestures came into popular use when our fighting forces—more than 8 million of them—brought them back. Words like *beaucoup* (pronounced "bow coo" by many, or "boo coo" where I grew up) and *voila* (pronounced "wa la" by much of the United States) are obviously French, but I'm willing to bet a lot of people, even though they may know that, have no idea how to spell them correctly. So World War II gave us common ground with many people from around the world, but that grip is starting to slide. Much like our Tower of Babel worker, that kind of commonality is morphing.

Indians use a lot of head gestures that Americans could easily misinterpret. Desmond Morris asserted that human beings' use of the nod is universal, going back to rubbing at the mother's nipple to get more milk. Not true. In Albania, people nod for "no." Indians rock their head from left to right rather than nod or shake. An Indian friend of mine told me that there are multiple head gestures to indicate acceptance, understanding, or disagreement, and that, during a conversation, much of the understanding is occurring through those movements. He said that non-Indian people might naturally have a difficult time grasping everything that is being communicated, particularly because others may associate different meanings with the movements.

If common hand and head signals can easily be confused, imagine the impact of more specialized signaling. Much of what children do in their natural play is what becomes gesture in a given location. This is the reason parents constantly attempt to teach their children that certain seemingly insignificant types of mimicry, as in this photo, are inappropriate for public display.

This innocuous signal would be found playful and amusing in our culture, but it cost Portugal's Economy Minister Manuel Pinho his

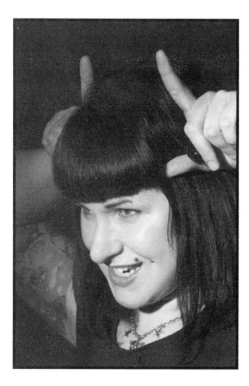

job in July 2009. This very piece of body language represents the cuckold insult in Portugal. If the word has no meaning to you it means a man whose wife sleeps around. He used this symbol during a state of the nation debate and directed the insult at Bernandino Soares, leader of the Communist parliamentary group. Note well that this is an example of engagement and focus behind a commonly understood action, and it generated an unmistakable message in that culture.

You may be still be thinking that this is just a goofy thing for this young woman to do, and that it would not likely happen in public. Here is another example of the cuckold signal; this one comes from Italy.

Again, this seems like a symbol you probably would not use in an everyday conversation. Think again. In some parts of the world, this signals "cuckold," but not for the students and fans of the University of Texas. To them, it's "hook 'em horns." People associated with the university or those

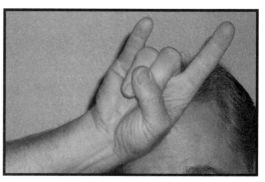

who support UT athletics use this same symbol—although not often placed in front of the forehead. Former President George Bush and his wife, Laura, signaled this during the Inaugural Parade and even later at the Inaugural Ball. The meaning is clearly understood among the University of Texas alumni, but imagine the potential misunderstanding for foreign onlookers.

There are only so many ways to gesture to send message, that it's amazing we ever get to a common understanding across culture. And, in fact, we often fail.

Using Culture to Block Understanding

Sometimes, people want to "fail" to communicate.

Street gangs and Masons aren't the only ones who use gestures to communicate privately, with the intention of not being understood by someone who does not belong to the culture.

The first time I got to the United Kingdom, I went straight to Ireland. Being polite, the British rail industry was on strike, but only every Tuesday. Why ruin every day for your fellow citizens; just ruin every Tuesday. And so I took a bus, which put me on the road to Wales, where I decided to stay for a few days. At the invitation of a pretty redhead I'd met on the bus, I made my way to a pub where she was a bartender. All around me, people were speaking Welsh and using hand signals that I still do not know the meaning of. I finally asked one of them, "Do you know when Brynn is coming in?" After he answered me, everyone in the bar started speaking English and stopped using the odd hand gestures. It was a tourist area, and locals relied on their Welsh tongue and gestures when they thought Brits were around. Once they realized I was American, they dropped them.

That kind of culture-specific communication can come out as a way of hiding messages or to be even more effective in communicating with your own kind.

On that same trip, I was driving around and found a tiny town in the middle of nowhere that was having a festival. A few of the local fisherman allowed me to hang out with them at a bar and drink Guinness. I could barely understand them because of their thick dialect. Finally, I understood that one of them was asking me how long I would be in County Cork. After hours of conversation, the bartender there did something that made the fisherman I had been talking with very, very angry. All I know is that it was about me and the exchange occurred through gestures that were inscrutable to me. The fisherman rose up to his full, imposing height and threatened the bartender. I said, "What going on?"

"He's being offensive to you."

"I didn't see anything," I said.

"That's because you're not from here." And then he went over the bar at the guy who had insulted me.

All of that quiet communication is a natural—and, paradoxically, both public and private—way of sending messages for many people in many cultures.

Signs of Alien Life

Take some basics you have learned in the last chapter and start to determine what we can understand *without* common gesture. Once again, let's return to this photo of Kofi. In the Introduction, you learned that he was gesturing about food. In Chapter 2, you saw only his hand moving toward the table as if he were making a simple point like "please pay attention to this next slide." Now take a look at the photo with an entirely open perspective.

Do you see any of the following:

a) Barrier? Closed eyes and movement to an oblique angle; there is also the table that serves as a barrier.

b) Adaptor? Are his feet tapping? What about his fingers and toes? Regardless of that, his left hand is gripping the chair arm, so we see at least one adaptor.

c) Regulator? Closing his eyes might be a regulator, depending on the conversation.

d) Illustrator? Does that desk-pounding action mean something specific? Is it congruent with the rest of his signaling?

Based on this photo, someone who is not from Ghana would probably still not know what he's trying to communicate. This is a set-up for a false cognate. Even with the involvement of the face, this looks like a common illustrator, such as something we see in meeting rooms around the world every day.

Re-create the body language for yourself and ask people who don't have the benefit of the explanation to tell you what they think it means. Imagine a bottle in your hand. Move your hand up and down, as though you are pounding the bottle on the table. Put a faint smile on your face while you do it. Did anyone you showed the gesture guess that it means "let's go get food" or "let's eat"? Even without their understanding of the gesture understood in Ghana, you could likely negotiate using common skills to ask why he is pounding the table. When you have only a photo for reference, you miss the opportunity to baseline and determine how all of the words in the body language sentence work together. In person, you get to negotiate the pieces you do not understand and to absorb meaning from context just as you would in spoken language.

Consider this photo of a man relaxing as he talks to the photographer. What does it mean that he puts his hands on top of his head as he talks? Is it a baseline? Relaxed? Comfortable? Reflective?

Now compare the two. Is there a difference? Only if you happen to understand the cultural signaling. Kofi's gesture, reflecting what his people do in Ghana, indicates the person you are talking about is dead. Greg is just relaxing.

This is the point of the display: Natural communication styles are inhibited by culture. You can develop a sense of style and body language all your own as long as it does not carry meaning that conflicts with the understanding of your audience. In that case you broadcast a message inadvertently that may not have anything to do with your intended signal.

Here is a scenario that's actually possible considering where these two men live and work. Greg meets Kofi in Atlanta, where they both have business. At a meeting where they are both present, Kofi thinks he's signaling that it's lunchtime. No one at the table tunes in except for Greg, who picks up that Kofi has something he wants to communicate. They negotiate language and body language and arrive at a common understanding. Greg responds and makes lunch happen. Six months later, Greg goes to Accra and happens to meet a member of Kofi's family. In relaying the story to Kofi's cousin, Greg feels relaxed, starts talking about Kofi, and puts his hands on his head. The message gets back to other members of Kofi's family that a friend of his from the United States came to tell them that he has died. It is the stuff of sitcoms.

Draw your own conclusions about this next gesture. According to Kofi, it means "get out"—but is this idiosyncratic to his tribal group, or does virtually everyone in Ghana recognize this gesture as "get out?" It could even be something idiosyncratic to his family, but, because he grew up responding to it and repeating it, to him, it represents a specific meaning that he associates with his culture.

Affecting Culture Through Gesture

Perception of your place in society and how normal you are in that society will play a part in how much confidence you have that you can use body language to mean something intentionally.

Probably all of our families have some weird little thing we do among each other to signal emotions, judgment, and so on. If your mother always put her hand on her hip when she found you aggravating, you could easily hang on to the perception for many years that "hand on hip" is a universal gesture that signals you have done something wrong. If you feel secure enough in your society, you may even pass that on to the people in your immediate circle— or, if you're a celebrity, to the world. You shift behavior, and, in some small way, you may shift thinking.

Entire communities sometimes deliberately assign new meanings to gestures as part of an attempt to change the behavior of a group. The generation that supported the Allies' efforts in World War II used the "V" signal with their fingers to signify victory. Their sons and daughters who opposed the Vietnam War co-opted the signal and gave it a new meaning: peace.

Churches aiming to present Jesus Christ as focused on spiritual matters and disregarding earthly ones have distorted a few pieces of his wisdom. For example, what was Jesus's intent in saying to his disciples: "But if anyone strikes you on the right cheek, turn to him the other also" (Matthew 5:39)? Think about which hand a person uses to strike you on your right cheek. It's the left hand—and in that culture and at that time (and it's no different now in parts of the world), the left hand was used for unclean tasks, whereas the right hand was used for eating. You touched animals and human waste with your left hand. The ultimate in passive resistance would be to force your assailant to treat you as a man and strike you with his right hand.

Returning to the straight-armed salute discussed at the beginning of the chapter, this is another example of a deliberate distortion of the meaning of a gesture to shift the thinking of those who either use it or see others who do.

Chapter 4

Scanning the Body Parts: The Head

People have the ability to send specific messages with each part of the body, just as a single word like *ouch!* can get a complete point across. Often, that will not be the case with body language. You will need to combine what the arms are doing with the action of brow and eyes, for example, and noticing whether the message matches what's coming out of the mouth. It's like listening to an entire sentence before you conclude what someone is saying. Each of these parts of non-verbal communication carries information. Like the elements of spoken language, each can be more or less important depending on context. For instance, a person covered in blood with multiple wounds would make better use of his dying breath uttering a proper noun than a verb. Similarly, sometimes a tap of the toe is a sign of boredom; other times, it's an incriminating message.

In observing individual movements as well as the whole picture, keep baseline in mind. In everyday life, not just on stage or in the movies, you see people who "overact." Their over-the-top style of expression may be part of their normal behavior. We develop patterns in our expression based on what we have been rewarded for; someone who grew up in a household with eight kids might have learned that exaggerated expression was the only way to get Mom's attention. If someone consistently uses that style, a deviation from baseline would be when he mutes the volume and becomes constrained in a situation where he would normally have been demonstrative. The opposite is true, too, so pay attention when a normally constrained person overacts, even with a single body part.

In this head-to-toe scan, I will start with the face, which Desmond Morris called the organ of expression. Morris conjectured it is the easiest to control because it is the closest to the brain—I strongly disagree. When it comes to the face, we have a paradox: The face is both the easiest and the hardest area of the body to control. We create many expressions with our faces that are second nature. We are unaware of doing them. Humans are pattern-seeking animals, and positive or negative reinforcement is a pattern. Temperament, nature, and nurture play a huge part in how we respond to that stimulus, and whether we use a given piece of body signaling or not. If Morris were right and we can control the muscles in the face more easily than others, then we wouldn't need cosmetic lifts, expensive creams, and Botox. We could voluntarily stop using the muscles that create creases, and reverse the process of wrinkling by exercising them. And if the face were under our control, more facial movements would be cultural—that is, intentional—rather than universal and unintentional.

The Face and Head

The face is a wonderfully complex set of muscles, bones, and nerves designed to communicate. In humans, muscles of the face attach to bone and skin, allowing us to make wild gestures and to control separate parts of the face independently. If you doubt this, stand in front of a mirror and make faces like you did when you were a child. While you are contorting your face, realize how awkward these expressions look on your current, mature face. That is because these wildly exaggerated distortions are things of the past for you. You have learned to link together each of the pieces of your face from jaw to scalp to send messages and signal in a way that is meaningful to others. As a result you have left muscle memory and patterning that you rely on to communicate. Some of this messaging is instinctive and universal, others a genetic remnant of your parents, and even some that is all yours. At any rate, you can learn what each piece of the face does independently. Remember, though: Just like the big four (illustrator, regulator, barrier, and adaptor), nothing is stand-alone. Your non-verbal voice is like a spoken language, and all of the pieces tie together to convey a message. Your face is an amalgam of its components when it comes to messaging.

Forehead

Your forehead not only serves as an important tool in communicating current messages, but it also gives clues about the messages you have sent in the past. You learn something about a person when you see lots of wrinkling on the forehead, and you learn something if you see none.

You can illustrate, regulate, and adapt by using the muscles in your forehead in different ways. In this chapter, you will learn to spot each type of expression quickly in addition to seeing other ways you use the brow region intentionally and unintentionally.

The complexity of what you can do with your brow to express both obvious and subtle messages makes it a valuable communication tool. Another type of complexity involves controlling the brow so that it does not show the obvious states such as excitement, surprise, anger, or pain, or the more subtle ones such as mild displeasure or curiosity. With each passing year, more layers of what you have felt and experienced are painted on the canvas in the form of wrinkles.

On the mature adult forehead:

Fewer than normal lines = your muscles have not had to work much.

More than normal lines = you are highly expressive.

No lines = you've had work done.

A person who has had Botox injections will have few to no lines on the face for her age. Someone who uses her brow dramatically and often will have higher than the normal amount of lines for her age. Genetics, thickness of the skin, sun and wind exposure, and the quality of moisturizer all can influence the appearance of wrinkles, but all they will do is affect the deepness of lines, not whether or not someone has them. A 50-year-old person with no wrinkling has almost certainly had some kind of cosmetic procedure or treatment—and I don't mean face cream and a few weekends at a spa. A person with nothing more than little wrinkling, perhaps only discernible to someone looking closely, is probably someone who just doesn't use the brow very much.

Most people are not conscious of how they use their forehead. My life as an actor, which is fundamentally what I was in interrogations, required me to do what any other actor would do: learn how to move the forehead to convey certain messages deliberately. A good friend of mine studied theater arts for many years, and one of the roles she played was Eliza Doolittle in George Bernard Shaw's *Pygmalion.* A look of surprise she inserted in her performance spontaneously at one performance got a big laugh. After that, night after night, she delivered that look at that moment. Every night, she got a laugh. If you ask her to do it today, decades later, she can still do it. And if you genuinely surprise her, her face looks just like that. It's just one of her "looks."

Actors aren't the only ones who have "rehearsed" looks like this. You may not consider your responses to various emotional situations practiced because you don't plan them, but in some ways they are. In the course of your life, you knit and furrow your brows in similar, or identical, ways over and over again. And your face shows it. Think of your mannerisms as a sort of dictionary of body language. In the same way your use of a new word stands out in your spoken vocabulary, using a new body language signal will look just as out of place.

Of course, there are good actors and bad actors. You've seen them: They do the same move over and over, and it's just wrong. You think, "I can play a despondent victim better than that" and you may be right, particularly if part of your daily life involves the role of despondent victim. The forehead, which many actors do not control well, will often give away their shortcomings in conveying emotions.

Kevin Spacey's portrayal of Roger (Verbal) Kint in the brilliant thriller *The Usual Suspects* (1995) illustrates the dramatic power of brow control. Kint calmly participates in an interrogation by U.S. Customs agent Dave Kujan (played by Chazz Palminteri) with an obvious *lack* of body language in his forehead area. Referring to himself as a CP (a person with Cerebral Palsy), Kint exhibits signs of both physical and mental deficits. His oddly immobile face projects a subhuman quality. When Kujan drops a shocking revelation into the conversation, Kint constricts the grief muscle in the middle of his forehead. (We wonder, of course, whether the surprise he appears to have is the information itself, or the fact that Kujan has it.) Later when Kujan mentions Keyser Söze, a notorious criminal, Kint explodes. Keyser Söze, synonymous with "the devil," is a powerful force, a source of fear and loathing. The logical conclusion that most audience members would draw from the outburst—showing uncharacteristic activity in the brow areas—is that shock produces involuntary and universal responses—that is, honest responses. That certainly was Kujan's conclusion, too. You might excuse the lack of Kint's previous expression by assuming he does not have the mental capacity to express feelings normally (hence the lack of brow movement), or he just mimics his prison buddies who stay cool under pressure. Regardless of which scenario is true, ballistic Kint seems like the real deal.

As the interrogation proceeds, Kint seems to develop a sense of comfort with Kujan. He has some life in his face as he tells stories. At that point, I got suspicious. My baseline for Kint indicated his normal expression was placid; he seemed deceitful when he used his brow in a typically "normal" way. Spacey's Kint soon appears to uncoil, losing his control as he talks about the shoot-out and expressing grief over the loss of his friend; there's a lot of brow action here. He even makes a disarming statement to Kujan that the reason he didn't run away was that he was afraid—and he accents it perfectly with raised eyebrows, the standard indication of "you believe me, don't you?"

At the end, we find out just how good an actor Kint is. Of course, we are not dealing with a real human being in Kint. We're seeing the output of a gifted actor, Kevin Spacey. He's the mastermind behind the brows that tell nothing and tell everything.

After reviewing some of Spacey's other movies, I would now assert that control over that usually uncontrollable part of the face is his stock-in-trade, an integral part of his talent. He acts from the brows down until the scene demands a show of emotion, and then he punctuates it with the appropriate brow movement.

What do these brow positions signal to you?

>> Brows straight up.

>> Brows down hard.

>> One brow arched.

>> Brows knit together in the center.

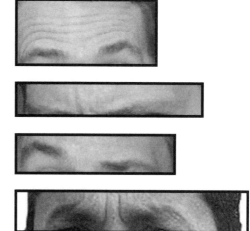

Is the brow signal alone enough to discern message? Try doing them yourself while looking in a mirror. Make a concerted effort not

to move anything else on your face. It's very hard. Though you will have a difficult time separating your brow from the rest of your face, you will clearly have the capability to discern certain families of emotions from brow movement.

A brows-up expression conjures ideas of uncertainty and questioning, although a hard ridge of a brow drawn down clearly indicates all doubt has been removed and not usually in good fashion. A clenched brow—meaning a drawing of the grief muscle—surely intimates some sort of concern, if not downright distress. So when you see one brow raised and the other drawn, it follows that you are seeing a person analyzing your offering for traces of deception.

Now, take a look through a mix of photos involving the brow and try first to categorize the feeling engendered by the brow alone. Try to focus on just the brow and leave the other elements out of your analysis.

Based solely on the brow, you can easily surmise that a rise of the brow straight up indicates new information, often unanticipated. This can be surprise, shock, or nearly any other form of sudden realization of the unexpected. Actually, seeing isn't necessary. Blind people will instinctively raise their brows when startled as well. In fact, being startled will cause many non-human and non-primate animals to raise their brows in response to the unexpected. An interesting aspect of human behavior is a universal flash of the eyebrows in recognition of those we know. We do it instinctively any time we see an acquaintance. It makes you wonder if we as a species are not somewhat surprised every time we see someone. If you "instinctively" know someone does not recognize you, it is because your mind's eye caught this bit of body language, or lack thereof, without your conscious knowledge.

If the muscles are clinched and involve the grief muscle, the message is very different. No amount of lower face contortion can hide the fact that a drawn-together brow even when lifted signifies distress or concern. Often in terror the brows can rise to a high point, but the grief muscle determines the difference between surprise and terror. Think of terrified as a cross between "I did not expect that" and "I wish I hadn't found it."

When someone drops his brow to a hard line as our model has done here, you have to look no further to understand that he is tak-

ing a hard line against something. If you were to change his lower features to a grimace, the message would be a more powerful one of anger instead of simply disapproval. Anger, disapproval, concern, and pain are a few of the states that can cause a person to pull down both brows. Most of these have one thing in common: negative energy. You can see it in these first three photos of Kurtis.

Any signaling that includes a dropped straight brow can be mitigated by other features, but it is difficult to create a positive message with this brow.

Seeing one brow up and one down brings a simple thing to mind. The brain is sending a dual signal. And because our brains are not good at intentionally sending a mixed signal, this is likely a natural response that becomes so encoded as a successful message that most of us use it. This is the standard eye raised for new input and one eye jaundiced as the still-out jury to determine whether or not the information has value.

Request for Approval

Another use of the brow is part of a complex body language expression I call "request for approval." Request for approval is the person asking *how* you perceive what he is saying, because he is unsure of where he stands, whether or not you believe him, or how an action is accepted. The eyebrows raise and hold, perhaps just momentarily—more than an "I recognize you" flash—but the amount of time is an eternity in terms of facial expression. You see the request for approval on a regular basis and even do it yourself when you are uncertain, but, until you can identify it as a discrete

gesture, you can only do it and respond to it instinctively, not cognitively. It is the brow version of raising the shoulders into a shrugging motion as a sign of helplessness. This alone is not an indicator that you are requesting approval, but is the fundamental element noticeable from a distance. Other elements of uncertainty tie into this total-body messaging, but its most prominent feature is the raised and held forehead.

Watch politicians during a press conference, stars on late-night talk shows, and students in a classroom for plenty of examples of the request for approval. Along with the expression, the person may also raise the pitch of her voice at the end of a sentence as if it were a question.

The brow can be used with full intent to convey any of these messages, and although you are likely not aware that you are signaling with your brow, the message you are sending is likely still intentional. Conscious use of the brow is a proactive tool that can allow you to drive a point more effectively or punctuate your thoughts more clearly than

words alone, especially when the use of hands is inappropriate. The brow can message "Do you understand?" You surely do not believe that!" "Enough! I am talking." and "Okay, it's your turn now." Even intentionally pausing can silently pose the question, "How do you perceive what I just said?"

Think of news talk show host Bill O'Reilly, who is adept at using his brow to control a conversation, drive home a point, stop banter, and signal that he doesn't believe something. On occasion, as his brow rises to a point of skepticism and he starts to dismantle an interviewee's story, he illustrates with his brows in downward motion to drive home his point about the guest's flawed logic. More than one person has probably left the show feeling "brow beaten."

The Brow and Grief Muscle in General

Someone under very high stress will often massage this muscle set between the eyes. This is often involuntary and an adaptor for high stress. Watch politicians as they get caught in their indiscretions; commonly, you will see them rubbing the area between their eyes. This is the same gesture that people with tension headaches commonly use. It's an involuntary response to the tightening of the muscles in that area—an unconscious attempt to stretch them and increase blood flow to the area.

The brow is a powerful illustrator, driving home its points and limiting other factors of the face from acting independently. It creases, wrinkles, and leaves behind traces of what you have done and how you have used it, further preventing you from casually changing your style. Used as it is designed, it can make points, ask for approval, signify recognition, disapprove, excuse, and even control the conversation. Just think of the brow as a large mechanical element of the face, with the eyes and mouth playing further key parts in demonstrating what is going on inside the person's head.

Eyes

Not only the eyes, but also the orbital sockets that the eyes operate in help us send messages. Among the primary changes in our anatomy from our other primate friends is enlarged sclera—that is, the white of the eye. The presence of sclera helps us to message each other with wide-open eyes to signal fear, and squinting to hide the sclera to indicate anger, for

example. The whites of our eyes are a very effective adaptation for humans to signal intentionally as well as unintentionally. Other elements of the eye structure play roles just as important. Consider the temples, pupils, and eyelids.

Temples

A genuine smile engages the temples. The eyes close a bit and wrinkles form at the edge of the eye.

The red-carpet smile that a lot of celebrities flash at awards ceremonies may be broad, but it's still fake. You also see a lot of

temple engagement in the brow action expressing negative emotions or concern.

In highly positive emotion, the muscles at the temple are the muscles that engage as primary drivers of the brow. That leaves the brow relatively slack in the middle and allows a pulping of the cheeks to create a fully happy smile. When the grief

muscle is engaged in any way, these muscles cannot effectively overpower the brow and the result is bizarre.

A quick look at musculature of the face shows muscles dedicated to facial movement. In addition to the many vari-

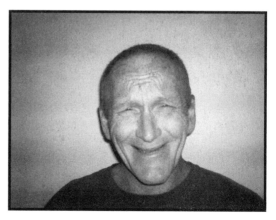

ations of expression these muscles can effect, the mobility of the jaw plays a huge part in facial appearance and can make someone seem rubber-faced. When muscles of the face draw and tighten, they plump just like flexing an arm bicep. As the muscles under the eyes in the center of the face bunch or flex to create a smile, the brow is typically relaxed and the muscles and other tissue create gentle wrinkling around the eyes. This is the hallmark of a real smile, because it is a smile that does not involve the brow in uncertainty or grief. Look at Brian in the photo at the top of page 97: His forehead is missing those characteristic wrinkles from earlier photos. The only real wrinkling now is at the temples or corners of the eyes, and of course his residual wrinkling.

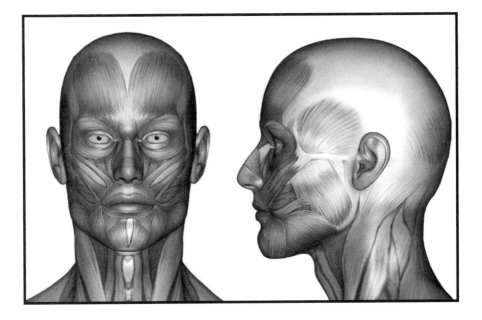

Pupils

Pupils naturally dilate for a number of reasons, including sexual attraction, fear, and curiosity.

The part of the peripheral nervous system called the sympathetic nervous system prepares us for fight or flight. The parasympathetic nervous system is a breaking mechanism that calms and places us in an un-aroused state. The arousal can be anytime we face an unknown circumstance or environment, or find ourselves in a situation we perceive as a threat.

When the sympathetic nervous system is engaged, your pupils dilate to take in more data about the threat. In less-technical terms, the pupils dilate when the brain needs more information than it currently has. If the brain thinks the object of focus is very good, such as someone sexually attractive, or the object appears dangerous, then the pupils will dilate. This is akin to identifying poisonous snakes by the shape of the pupil: When you are close enough to see it, you are committed. Other pieces of body language clarify why the person has dilated pupils. Anger, sexual attraction, and fear all have very distinct signaling in other parts of the body, so the holistic being looks very different, though the pupils are sending the same signal.

This photo shows Brian looking at the photo of an attractive young woman in tight clothing. The fact that his pupils dilate when looking at her indicate she is sexually interesting.

If the brain is disinterested or repulsed, the pupils will pinpoint to shut it out. In a normal state, your pupils are neither dilated nor pinpointed. They are somewhere in between. When pupils flash, the sympathetic and parasympathetic nervous systems are in conflict. The sympathetic dilates; the parasympathetic relaxes or pinpoints. Flashing can be continuous, or a quick flash and then gone. Both excitement and stress can cause this kind of pulsing.

Eyelids

Often when there are clichés in society, their foundation has been part of human culture since before written history. The fluttering eyelids and lashes of the "dames" from film noir of the 1940s is a good example. We use our lids to communicate in numerous ways. From the simple "go away" close of the eyes to the sophisticated approach taken by former Senator Jeremiah Denton, author of *When Hell Was in Session,* human beings have devised ways to use the eyelids with intent and power. In a 1966 television interview, Denton was forced to give an interview while he was being held prisoner by the North Vietnamese. Denton ingeniously seized the chance to communicate with American Intelligence. During the interview, he blinked in Morse Code to spell out the word "t-o-r-t-u-r-e," thus communicating that his captors were torturing him and his fellow POWs.

In relation to just the eyelids, think about the big four: illustrators, barriers, regulators, adaptors.

ILLUSTRATORS

Like Kofi's signal to go away, the lid can be used to illustrate a point clearly. Although this expression can often include the brows, a simple closing of the eyes indicates you are not pleased, annoyed, frustrated, or other signals delivering the message "go away." In order to convey any other message with eye closing, you need additional signals. So, although closing your eyes and smiling can indicate you were taken by surprise by a punch line, closing your eyes with a straight, smile-less face conveys something more akin to "why are you bothering me?"

Fluttering eyelids (not taken to the extreme) can serve as an intentional indication that you are interested in a person. This is a corruption of the body's natural tendency to blink more as excitements takes hold of the body. Eyelids can also illustrate a point by closing to exaggerate the difficulty of a decision a person is making. Often this closing of the eyelids is more of a squint by one or both eyes. Many people also wink to illustrate they have made a sarcastic, funny, or astute observation. A wink can just as easily indicate that you are talking to an insider who knows something others do not.

The lids can be used in more permutations than are possible to illustrate in words or even photographs because people adapt ways to tie the eye movement into their daily lives. Lid movements can signal easily because we are so focused on the eyes.

BARRIERS

One style of answering tough questions that may be cultivated or occur naturally includes pausing, exhaling, and closing the eyes before responding. If that is a baseline normal for the person, then everything is okay, but she will likely arouse the suspicions of any person who hasn't seen it before. We instinctively, at least in American culture, like eye contact. Pulling down the shades indicates someone might be "pulling the wool over our eyes." Blinking and therefore closing the eyes is a natural response to stress and purely physiological.

When you become stressed to the point of fight or flight, the sympathetic nervous system kicks in, and one result is that your body steals blood from less important parts such as mucous membranes. When mucous membranes lose blood flow, they start to dry. These membranes line all of the smooth, moist parts of the body such as the inside of the eyes and mouth, and, when they begin to dry, you blink to rewet the eyes and lick your lips. So if your blink rate is higher than normal for you, then something has engaged the sympathetic nervous system. Blinking to rewet your eyes is like dragging a wet cloth over them. As your eyes feel drier and drier, you drag the cloth more often. The problem is that the cloth isn't really wet after a short while, so the dragging causes you to blink even more. People instinctively know something is wrong with another person when the patterns for blink rates change; almost every person who sees video of increased blink rate has rising suspicions. It might indicate nothing other than stress, but sometimes that is enough. With sustained stress the lids become thin and drawn as the mucous membranes dry out even more. The result is that more of the whites of the eyes

show, and it may even extend to the point that the lower sclera might become visible. Like high blink rates, drooping lower lids may be nothing but normal for a person, but if not, then this is a sure sign of stress.

Closing the eyes altogether also indicates something if it's not the person's habit. If he only blocks your line of sight in times of hard issues, for example, it can be an indicator that he needs more space. It will likely be accompanied by physical adaptors if this is the case.

REGULATORS

The flutter of eyelids from an attractive woman broadcasts "I want to hear more" to a man who has been telling her his life story.

Lids can also stop a conversation. Using partially closed lids to barrier during an unpleasant story, especially if accompanied by the drop of the forehead, would do the job. The signal usually must be understood to regulate conversation, so the squint of both lids as you listen will clearly indicate that the details of the story are painful to listen to; closing one eye and tilting your head would accomplish the same thing. This can be cultural, as you have seen from Kofi using the Ghana "go away" gesture, as depicted on the previous page. Though Kofi's message is "go away," you do not need to be Ghanaian to understand this is a regulator.

ADAPTORS

Adaptors are the most unique components of human body language. Any individual can use the lids to create a move that regains a measure of control. Remembering that adaptors are as individual as people, you simply need to look for a pattern. When I was a kid in south Georgia, there was a very old-South woman I knew well who would close her eyes fully and flutter her lids around in times of conflict. In those days, I just thought it was odd. Now I realize that open conflict was outside of her comfort zone and that the eye-close and flutter were how she dealt with that discomfort—clearly an adaptor.

Sexuality

The opposite of a fight-or-flight response occurs in times of sexual attraction. Rather than blood flow leaving the mucosa, it increases dramatically to the areas that provide sexual stimulation. When blood floods the mucosa of the eyelids the lids become heavy, and "bedroom eyes"—heavy-lidded, droopy, but not sleepy, eyes are the result. Look at these two examples of the same young woman at baseline and aroused. Can you identify the difference? And not just by where she is looking.

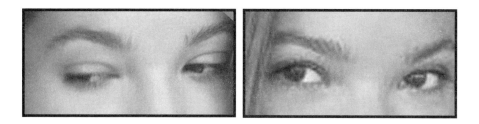

The cosmetic appearance of the eyelid also affects sexuality. Excess skin around the eyes, even when it occurs in a young person, has an aging effect. The person appears sleepy and older than her years. People with naturally baggy eyes look tired, or even sad. Sagging upper lids and puffy lower lids broadcast problems. Others might commonly conclude that they are people of extremes: too much alcohol, not enough sleep, or too much fat in their diet. For the person who has this condition, it can contribute to some very self-conscious body language associated with those judgments about lifestyle. In assessing someone's body language, be sure to consider energy level, focus, and other holistic considerations addressed in greater depth later in this handbook.

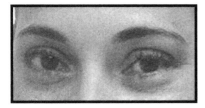
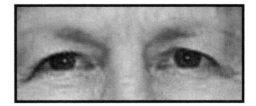

Eye Movement

Many Americans believe they know when someone is lying. When asked what is the number-one indicator someone is lying, most will say that the person breaks eye contact. So let's test that theory. Take a minute to answer this question out loud and pay attention to what your eyes do as you answer.

> Describe the library or media center in
> your elementary school.

You likely found your eyes moving around as you struggled to remember some of the details, or maybe even any details, of what the room looked like. Eye movement signals you are thinking. The myth about breaking eye contact as a sign of lying has been passed on by parents, teachers, and other people who heard it from a "reliable source" and just passed it along. Evasion of eye contact is different from looking around as you think—that's an important distinction, and the one element of the broken-eye-contact myth that holds true. Because most people are looking around as part of the thinking process, the only time you probably notice others' eye contact is when you are looking for it, which is probably little more than half the time. It's natural to believe that any less means the person is lying.

The references to brain structure that follow aren't meant to convince you I have expertise in neurobiology; they are simply useful references. I assume the eye follows brain activity and blood flow, and that means the eye movement is easy to pattern. In discussing what eye movement means, "left," means the person's left; same for "right."

The visual cortex is in the back of the brain, so if your eyes are going to follow blood flow, you would imagine your eyes would look very high up, and you would be right. When a person is accessing a visual cue, he will look up higher than his brow bone. Because sound is processed just above the ears, as you would expect the eyes to go somewhere between the brow ridge and cheekbone for auditory clues. There are two other rules that always appear to be the same; let's address those straightforward rules later after covering the complex ones governing eye movement related to visual and auditory accessing.

Typically, we associate logic and reasoning with the left side of the brain. This is why we call logic-driven people "left-brained." We typically associate the right brain with creativity and imagination, and therefore refer to artists and artsy people as "right-brained." So when a person is asked to remember the detail of Helen the Librarian's clothing styles, she typically would look to the place she stores memories (left side of the brain), and, because it is a visual cue, the eyes would move to above the brow ridge, like the woman in the photo following on page 106.

If I asked a question like "How do I get to the nearest grocery store from your house, and please include landmarks to help me find it," I would expect to see that kind of eye movement. Both she and the man are responding with the same basic move—one is simply posed as he recalls days gone by, his body part of the overall movement—the other using only her eyes. The question must ask the person to recall a specific visual detail, and it must require thought, not a simple fact that is easily regurgitated.

Follow that with a question that requires a visual creation—that is, imagination focused on something he has never seen—and the eyes will move upward, but in the opposite direction. "What does the surface of Jupiter look like?"—if he really tries to give a thorough description—will involve reaching to the visual center, above the brow ridge and probably up right.

Now for the complication: A small percentage of people are wired exactly the opposite, so when they are asked a visual memory question they will go up (above the brow) and to their right for a visual memory instead of up and to the left. This is unrelated to handedness.

How do you know when someone is wired opposite and not just answering your question with purely fabricated details? Baseline. Ask a question you know the answer to and watch which way the person accesses to determine what is normal for him. For instance, you might ask details from a meeting that you supposedly forgot, or inquire who won the latest season of *American Idol*. You can baseline and he is none the wiser.

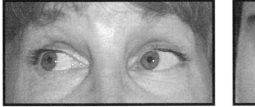 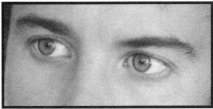

Eye movement in response to auditory cues follows the same pattern as visual: In general, it's left for memory and right for creative. The difference is that auditory cues are between the brow ridge and cheekbone. More importantly, the sides never cross; so, if a person remembers visual cues to his left, he will remember auditory clues to his left as well. The kinds of questions that work for determining auditory baseline are asking about lyrics to a popular song or details from a conversation.

 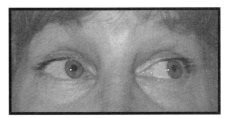

Just like in these photos, some people will have more of a degree of movement depicted and some less, but the movement will be clearly evident to you. As someone recalls an issue and you ask questions, she might bring the subject back into focus as the eyes look straight ahead, analyzing and answering questions, or the eyes might continue dancing from place to place depending on the individual's baseline.

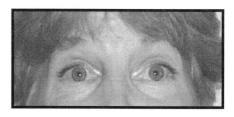

Also realize that you need to keep the sensory channel questions pure by asking questions that are factual, and separate auditory from visual cues. Stay away from questions that evoke feelings or you will get into one of the other two constants: emotion.

Think of the emotional side of our brains as a combination of our intellectual capacity (to link situations, entitlement, reputation) and

our animal response from the mammalian brain. This means that the very part that makes us human—our frontal cortex—is engaged. When this happens and we become emotional, our eyes drift down and to the right.

Emotions can be sadness, or any other really intense emotional feeling. These emotions can cause us to even shift our entire head down and to the right, meaning our postures and movement are impacted. Other animals become emotional, but not usually with the complexity that a human does. Emotion is always the same down and to the right (the individual's right).

The last of the signals is a gift of our frontal cortex. When a person engages in inner voice conversation or works through a problem with cognitive deliberation she will look down and to the left (the individual's left). There is an anomaly related to eye movement as well. Supposedly, none of these rules apply to the Basque people, native to the Northern Iberian Peninsula. After questioning a man of Basque parents I believe this must be related to native language patterning the brain. He had a clear and discernable pattern in line with that of the majority of people.

Center of the Face

Many people recommended I see *Beowulf,* a 2007 film employing "motion capture process," because they were so impressed with the true-to-life movements of the animated characters. Focusing on arms, legs, and torso—the movements of which were captured very well—they missed something key. It is tough to watch the movie for more than 10 minutes at a time, because one significant type of body language is missing: movement in the center of the face. The drawing on page 110 showing the layers and interplay of muscles in the face illustrates how much muscle there is around the cheekbones. The muscles between the lower orbital and upper jaw line take an active role in your smile, smirk, and other twists and turns you do with your mouth, nose, and eyes. The lifeless appearance of the center of the *Beowulf* characters' faces gives the sense that they have two faces—eyes upward and mouth downward—connected by a dead zone. If you were to see a person walking down the street who presented expression that way, you would probably think he was mentally disturbed.

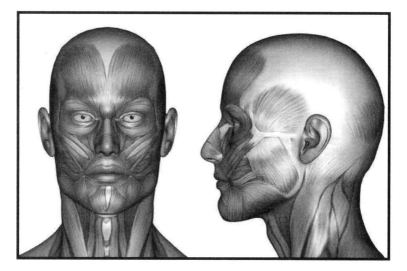

This center-of-the-face action is in fact so key that most good interrogators who prefer not to be read instinctively leave the center of the face inanimate.

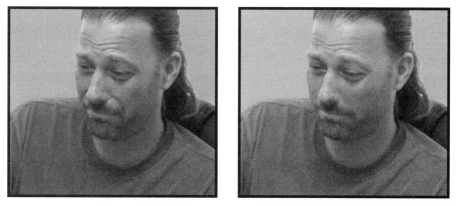

In Chapter 2, you first saw this photo of Brian displaying disgust. Compare it to the retouched version on the right that removes some of the action in the center part of his face. It's like an instant facelift—and if you don't know what happens if a facelift is too extreme, just use your hands to pull back the skin and take a look in the mirror. The center part of the face has little or no action.

Say this series of words and, while you do, pay attention to what part of your face moves in addition to your mouth: maggot, vomit, bloodthirsty. Words like these that evoke an emotional response in addition to forcing the mouth to move necessarily engage muscles in the center of the face. When you watch an animation in which only the lips form words like this, on some level, you know that does not look authentic.

Look at the entire group of muscles depicted in the illustration one more time and realize how key each is to everyday facial expressions. A grimace that engages muscles along the jaw line and drags down the corners of the mouth naturally also drags down the muscles that gather around the eyes in a natural smile. When the brow draws to a point in the center of the head it drags along with it any semblance of a normal smile. Muscles in the center of the face are crucial to communication and yet an afterthought for the most sophisticated of animators.

Human faces are complex, and once a person learns a given expression is an effective communication and uses it a few times, other muscle combinations get tougher. Stand in front of a mirror and attempt to engage the grief muscles while smiling. The results are a complicated and mixed message, as you can see on this little girl's face. Is she  happy or worried? Look at the photo taken apart.

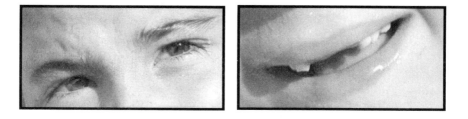

You could learn to contort your face, but the messages you send would be received poorly. Muscle memory like this is a key to getting the real message people are sending, even when they have no idea it is there.

Some combinations are learned and peculiar to an individual. But going back to Ekman's basic, well-documented facial expression, here is a good example of one that is hard-coded to our collective psyches.

The flexing of the muscles in the cheeks in this photo of an adult woman creates rounding, as in a smile, but the pinching affect of those muscles—as if to protect the olfactory glands from something unpleasant—draws the muscles

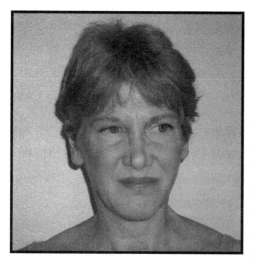

into a narrow center. This is the face of displeasure. Eyes can be open or closed, but the wrinkling of the nose, drawing of the grief muscle, and tightening of the lips together signal disapproval and disgust. She may moderate some of the muscle action and convey the same expression, but the minute she toys with the fundamentals of the signal, the message is lost.

Given a situation that limits full expression, like the look of your mother-in-law's prized gizzard casserole, you probably find a way to mitigate your reactions: You "grin and bear it." This will come into play dramatically when you are trying to hide your body language or find someone else's hidden body language.

Nose

Although not the most mobile of facial features, the nose can still play a huge part in signaling both intentionally and unintentionally.

In the unintentional category, when in fight or flight, the nostrils flare to take in more air. This is primarily a response to increases in the metabolic rate to prepare the body for action. Wrinkling the nose is another example. A quick review of musculature shows we all have the capability to wrinkle the nose, and every one of us does it involuntarily to varying degrees to signal disgust, rage, and sometimes even uncertainty or skepticism.

In the intentional category, the nose can be used independent of whole-face signaling. Women often use a nose wrinkle when amused or questioning. Some women can also use the nose as a regulator in conversation, again just by using a little wrinkle to suggest displeasure with whatever is being said.

The nose wrinkle that little boys use as a signal all but disappears in adult males, although it is retained in universal signaling of disgust. Some men might still retain nose wrinkling as a messaging tool if their primary role models and people they communicate with most often are women. Like other signaling, facial expressions are affected by the people we communicate and identify with.

The nose is a cluster of blood vessels and nerves. As a result, any time a person feels stress and blood flow increases, the nose seems to be one of the first places to itch. The itching can become so pronounced that a person cannot stop touching her nose. Often the itching is associated with the inside of the nose as mucosa dry out— but remember that sometimes an itch is just an itch. Look for other unintentional signals of stress like thin lips, white skin, and dilated pupils to get a complete picture reflecting stress. Concurrently, look for an increase in barriers and adaptors.

Brow/Mouth Combinations

A great deal of the brow's message depends on the position of the mouth, a body part that will be covered in greater detail later in the chapter. For now, just focus on the combination of a few mouth positions with the brow. One of the commonalities among the different types of expressions is that the action of the brow can be used to minimize the amount of data that can come into the eyes. This is a forehead movement, therefore, that you would not associate with something positive.

> ▸▸ When the brows drawn down combine with the corners of the mouth pulled down, and the nose crinkles, that's a look of disgust. Refer back to Chapter 2 and the look of disgust depicted there. You see the relationship of brow and mouth most clearly in Brian's face (center photo, page 53) because his face has the creases of someone who is habitually expressive. The same combination is evident to some degree in both of the others, with the big difference in brow expression relating to the broadness of the brows of both Kofi and the girl. Their bone structure stretches the muscles differently than on Brian's face.

>> Disapproval or displeasure would involve a downward push of the brow and a drawn mouth that's almost a sneer.

>> In a look of pain, a person may have the drawn brows become part of the action to keep the eyes closed.

Ears

The main signal you get from ears is flushing. Ears often flush at the onset of embarrassment and when people are lying. Bluffing being a variation of lying, you might look for flushed ears at the poker table.

You can also tell something about age from ears, which keep growing through life and sag, just like the rest of us. The ears are also high adaptor tools, primarily because the ears are so sensitive that people stroke, touch, fondle, gouge, and even tug the ear as a nervous action. This can become such a ritual that the person no longer realizes he is doing it. One man I worked with would tug his ear when in deep thought. A clear signal for him sitting in the office was grasping his ear, eyes down left (calculation/cogitation), even when no one else was in the room. When ear-tugging gets to that point, it can become idiosyncratic behavior, but that doesn't diminish its value to you in understanding his body language. In baselining this individual, you would notice it is part of his repertoire. It's part of how he operates.

Mouth

Most universal messaging involves the mouth. From disgust to anger to sadness to joy, all involve signaling with the mouth so naturally that emoticons are possible. The mouth is the primary organ of communication for most people who can speak. When the words coming out of it alone are not conveying the message, the natural adjunct is to position it to regulate, adapt, and illustrate. Occasionally, people even use it to barrier.

BARRIERS

A person who feels uncomfortable about his teeth (and this is an American obsession), whether due to straightness or color, will often use his lips to cover the teeth. In the same way physical barriering means "I need more space," he is looking for cover for his less-than-prized teeth. This can result in a closed-mouth, non-committal smile until absolute joy erupts. People who are being secretive might take

the same approach, so you need to know what is normal for the person. If his teeth are crooked and he is self-conscious, he will likely cover his teeth, but that does not automatically mean he isn't being secretive. Clusters of other indicators can mean that, although he always barriers his teeth, this time it is voluntary to hide clandestine conversation.

Another opportunity to barrier comes primarily from men in the form of a lip grip. Men will sometimes purse and grip their lips so their lips almost disappear. Often, that is a man holding back emotion, and it is an expression that made the front page of many newspapers in the summer of 2009. Following statements about the arrest of an African-American professor by a white police officer, President Barack Obama realized he had not monitored his words as carefully as he'd wished. The photo that made the news was Obama in a lip grip.

Children use their mouths like little hands, scooping up every object of curiosity. Adults quickly stop that and turn them into functioning adults. But one thing we never seem to remove from our children is the use of the mouth when thinking. If you have ever watched a child color or struggle with a task, you have seen the lips smacking or tongue run outside the mouth. Humans are not the only animals that do this. Other mammals like horses have high mouth involvement when learning a new task. Although most of us lose the lip smacking and licking, very few lose altogether the mouth involvement in thinking. In some people, it can remain as phantom chewing as they ruminate, and in others it becomes simply a  movement of the jaw or mouth almost like chewing the inside of the lip. Others will run the tongue over the teeth to get the same effect.

As an illustrator, the mouth plays a regular role. When someone slows to speak and over-enunciates, he is making a point not only with the verbal, but also the non-verbal voice. It punctuates thoughts like "How dense are you?"

Baring the teeth can take two forms: a grimace or a smile. The meanings are dramatically different in rage or anger, with the teeth bared in full array ready to broadcast the message clearly—much as a predator would bare its teeth at prey. Most people are less than conscious of the appearance of their teeth when they are angry for two reasons. First, they are not seeking approval. Second, when they get to this point, the mammal rather than cognitive portion of the brain is in charge and the person is reactive instead of thinking.

For most of us the difference is striking, but think about why. In a positive expression, the upturn of the mouth removes the brow from the equation, thereby relaxing the upper face. The center of the face is engaged and plumped, and the teeth are put on display more as a sign of health than a display of weaponry. This showing of

the teeth is one that is caused by the middle of the face drawing the upper lip to uncover the teeth.

Just as the entire face is involved in real smile, the whole face is involved in real rage. It takes specific effort to uncover the teeth for purposes other than these and sublime effort to cover the teeth during these two emotional states. People always associate rage with interrogation; as a result, when an interrogator wants someone to be clear that he is being interrogated, the interrogator displays rage. Most often the display is to hide much more subtle psychological approaches an interrogator is taking with words. All young interrogators can get the nuances of rage right.

Negative Signaling

Pursed lips are commonly used by women to indicate disapproval. Remember your

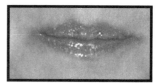

high school librarian giving you one of these looks before telling you to "shhh!"

Men have the same amount of control with a different look. The intent is the same—disapproval. No matter how you mask it, the message is clear.

In revulsion a person can draw in the lower lip and jaw to the point that the lower lip rolls over. The effect is a look as if someone is about to vomit.

A sarcastic smirk can also clearly send a message of disapproval, skepticism, or downright condemnation. Few human beings need to be told this: A sarcastic smirk from one man to another can easily create an uncomfortable, if not violent, outcome.

Lips thrust forward can indicate absolute disapproval. Think of the 4-year-old angrily pulling his lips together and thrusting them forward as he screams, "No!"

The sideways twist of the lips often indicates outright skepticism.

A fully opened mouth with a slack lower jaw clearly indicates surprise or shock and tells you to look to the upper face for more clues.

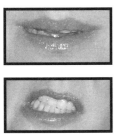

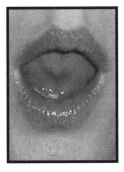

You will get distinct clues about a person's state by looking at whether the ends of the mouth are drawn up, down, or straight across. Combined with the brow, the mouth position can give you an entire, accurate reading of an emotion.

As I mentioned before, in a fight-or-flight situation, the body forces blood to the big muscles to prepare them for action, so the face loses blood. One effect is that the lips look thinner than normal. In contrast, sexual arousal will direct blood to

the face, with the effect being that lips, cheeks, and eyes look softer and rounder. Look at his example of a young man and a woman before and after intimate contact. Though this is clearly a staged photograph, the arousal is evident. Lips, noses, and lids are fuller and more involved. The difference is striking.

Before the "plumping technology" that exists now to shoot collagen and hydration into the lips to give them a fuller look, women commonly bit gently on their lips to stimulate blood flow and give them a little extra color and fullness.

Covering the mouth is a barrier with many possible meanings. Because a number of factors could be behind masking the teeth with lips or hands, knowing the context is key to your interpretation. Why would anyone cover her mouth?

» Trying to eat and talk at the same time, which is not considered appropriate in many cultures.

» Self-conscious about her teeth.

» Shy; uncomfortable with smiling broadly.

» Throwing up a barrier while divulging a secret or attempting to speak without being discovered.

Desmond Morris speculated that humans stick out their tongue as an automatic rejection of something, and tracked that behavior to an infant thrusting the tongue against the mother's breast when he doesn't want any more milk. After pondering this and observing people in different circumstances, I think he's right. When it's an unintentional action, as opposed to a deliberate expression, pushing the tongue out of the mouth seems to be an action of avoidance or rejection.

As a final note on the mouth, look to the lines around the mouth to see what the person normally does with it. If the lines tell one story and her expressions another, be skeptical. The lines did not get there by accident, so a person with a huge smile and laugh lines is going to use her face in animated fashion when happy. If she gives you a mediocre smile, she is demonstrating a mediocre feeling. If her face is line-free, then the best that you should hope for in terms of a smile is a mildly amused look.

Jaw

A jaw might be set, thrust forward, slack, or in a natural position. A set jaw and raised head are a defiant, and perhaps confrontational, combination.

When people feel indignant, entitled, arrogant, or justified, they will raise the jaw, throat exposed, almost as if saying, "Go ahead. I have nothing to hide. I am right and justified and you cannot take that away from me." It is often misunderstood as arrogant if a person carries his head high. You need to look past the jaw line for other indicators to understand the meaning. Arrogance often has a smirk or sarcastic smile. Indignance has a smile-less face, and defiance—a bit of a scowl.

When people feel defeated, hopeless, disgraced, or consumed by something beyond their control, they will drop the chin to cover the throat almost as if they are not justi-fied and do not want to go out this way. The photo shown here is a person consumed by a headache. In an interrogation, a good inter-rogator recognizes a very similar expression. It is the hopeless look of a person about to confess—a person defeated, disgraced, and caught. A person defiantly confessing with his head up is likely delivering a false con-fession. Seeing the distinction is one of the tools of a scrupulous interrogator.

Just as people have a tendency to move their eyes in search of images, sounds, and answers, many people have a tendency to move their jaws as they search for words. This kind of jaw movement could also serve as a regulator. You see it and recognize that the person doing it wants to say something.

Head and Neck

To separate the head and neck in terms of signaling is impos-sible. Head signals are done by the neck; the head is just a huge weight waiting to have the neck muscles make it move. Most sig-naling accomplished by the head/neck combination is illustrating, regulating, and gesture.

The neck can whip the head around in clarifying points to punctu-ate a thought, as in the traditionally feminine movement to illustrate frustration. The neck can also crane forward to indicate interest and focus. When someone is keenly interested, his head and neck may push forward to get closer to the action. In anger, frustration, and defiance, the person will often crane his neck forward to push at you with his signaling.

Distancing with the head and neck when someone is not allowed to get up and leave a situation can become almost comical. The amount of distance a person can contrive by moving his head to the back or front or side is the stuff of cartoons. The neck can be used to indicate amusement to roll the head away with the face in a smile or open-mouthed laugh.

The head thrown back

with a sigh and a scowl indicates exasperation. The neck is being used to get away from the source of frustration.

When someone is thinking, he might crane his neck to odd positions as he moves his eyes around his head. This is a purely unintentional signal that can be discerned in the same way you discerned the connection between eye movement and visual or auditory accessing. Head tilts often correspond with the eye movement, so that a down-right look of someone in a state of deep emotion, for example, may also involve the entire head plunging down right. You often see this posture at funerals. In this photo, Kofi uses his whole head as he struggles to recall something he wanted to relate about his homeland. Head tilts or head bobs may also serve as illustrators to reinforce a statement or substitute for it.

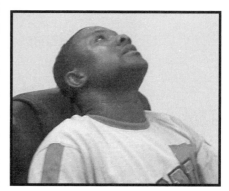

Tilting the head can substitute for eye movement or compound eye movement. As Kofi tried to recall details about the last time he was in Ghana, his head went back and his eyes rolled further up as if the more dynamic attempt would help him to recall. That's a natural thing to do.

Often people in highly emotional states will drop their entire heads down and to the right. When in this state, posture and movement in addition to all other body language is impacted. The person will likely communicate less. High emotion typically involves a cause, and the cause can be consuming. Sometimes as people move their heads, their eyes remain static. You will need to baseline everyone with eye movement questions to determine to what degree they use head and eye movement normally.

Movement of the head can also be a cultural gesture, as in the way Indians use a gentle rocking of the head left to right to signify affirmation, whereas most of the Western world uses the nod and shake to signal yes and no. Some less evident, but equally used, in American culture are the following:

>> A sharply cocked head serves as a challenge, suggesting "You don't know what you're talking about," and is usually accompanied by a skeptical facial expression.

>> Nodding your head to get someone to talk more. This is often instinctive, but if you have never used this, be sure to try it. People assume you understand and agree, and will continue to talk.

>> Shaking your head to get someone to stop talking.

>> Tilting the head as if to ask "what?"—particularly when combined with knit brows that suggest confusion.

>> People instinctively hold their necks rigid in times of uncertainty. It is as if they are afraid to convey any message by bobbling the head about for fear of messaging yes or no. The face is still alert, but the neck remains stationary.

Thanks to the neck muscles that give the head mobility to tilt and twist, the head can easily be used to signal intentionally in illustrating and regulating. You can point with your head to say "your turn" or beckon with a motion to "come here." You can baton or drive home your points with a downward slam of the forehead.

Pain and discomfort associated with the neck create adaptors as people touch, pet, and rub the neck and shoulder to relieve stress. The tension of the neck they are trying to relieve can itself be a clear signal that the topic is not pleasant or, at the very least, demanding a lot of thought. This is one of the most misread pieces of body language in law enforcement, where people often mistake this for a pre-violence pose. This is really an indicator of stress or something that takes a lot of mental focus.

One last note about the neck: In women the neck and upper chest can blotch in response to stress in social or work settings. Intimate settings can bring this result, too, but as a response to very, very good stress.

Total Face

Desmond Morris called the face the organ of communication, and I agree with him on that. He also postulated that we have more control over the face than any other part of the body because the face is closer to the brain and under more control. In variation from Morris, I believe the face is so often used we are unaware of what it does and with what frequency. Looking at the combinations of jaw, forehead, and center of the face, you can quickly understand that the face is our most complex canvas. When we give way to unbridled emotion and express exactly what we think using the face, all of the subtleties and nuance will come through. The reality is that few of us are allowed to act as though we are 4 years old. We learn to mask. Like a bodybuilder turned ballet dancer, we can only do so much to mask our background.

In reading body language, you are not going to find the 4-year-old's expression, except on a 4-year-old. You are going to find remnants of the 4-year-old, though, depending on the person's place in the hierarchy of your society. How you fit and where you fit into your different communities play an important part in how you opt to use the face you were given. If you have a large jaw and prominent cheekbones, the leveraging of muscles can create sharp contrasts from expression to expression. If you have a smaller jawbone and less-pronounced cheeks, the result is a fleshier and less dynamic canvas. Regardless of what you feel you should do now, you may have gotten used to doing something previously. After repeated use, muscle memory condemns us all to being deciphered. The real magic for you as someone who is becoming skilled in reading body language is in opening your eyes and looking for those remnants.

Chapter 5

Scanning the Body Parts: Shoulders to Toes

Shoulders

As we move to the shoulders, an important reminder: There are no absolutes, and the intent of this book is to allow you to learn to read body language, not simply jump to conclusions.

Posture is a good indicator of two things: culture and grooming. For Americans, standing tall with square shoulders is an indicator of integrity. Squared shoulders on a man or woman convey control and alertness, which is why the U.S. military requires that stance. Of course, physiology dictates exactly to what extent a person can assume the position.

Whether squared or not, you can pick up a lot from shoulder positions:

▶▶ Exaggeration of the squareness of the shoulders can indicate insecurity. Often when a man feels insecure he will square his shoulders forward and flex his back in an attempt to look more physically threatening.

» When fight or flight strikes, the shoulders naturally go back and draw to prepare for battle.

» Shoulders that are elevated to present the appearance of up, not squared, can indicate nervousness and uncertainty.

» Drooping shoulders can indicate defeat and are sometimes used intentionally to signal an overall body language of defeat.

» A quick, intentional droop can be a deliberate signal of exasperation—that is, "I am fed up." This movement is usually accompanied by a sigh, rolling of the eyes, and head rolled back.

» The number-one signal for helplessness is shrugged shoulders with palms up. Most Americans instinctively recognize this one.

» When someone is under high stress, he might also shrug his shoulders as an adaptor.

Arms

Chapter 2 began by introducing the most prevalent misconception about body language: that folded arms mean someone is blocking you out.

Barriers

In the following pictures, though all have arms crossed, only two of them seem to need space. Can you identify the two? And more importantly, based on the combination of other body signaling, why do they probably want more space?

The man on the left looks confident and attentive with the arms crossed as likely more of a comfort or assertion move, and he shows little insecurity and clear focus on something. His slightly amused smile and chin up indicate comfort if not a hint of pride as perhaps he listens to a message he agrees with.

The woman is clearly barriering, but it isn't likely she needs space because of insecurity; it's more likely out of annoyance. She wants to put distance between her and you. The evasion of eye contact and messaging with the mouth are a dismissive message. You can even imagine her right foot tapping as a combination of regulator and adaptor, as in "Can we just end this?"

The man in the black shirt indicates discomfort; his shoulders are up and tense, his grief muscle engaged, and his neck stiff. He is using the barrier to get more space.

The man in the suit accompanied by two others is not barriering for more space, but to send a message that the jury is out on your statement. Notice the slightly tilted head and squinted eyes as he turns his cognitive ability to you. One good rule of thumb: If the arms are gripped tightly to the body and not relaxed, it is not a baseline; it is a barrier.

The arm does not have to cross the torso to create a barrier. This photo of a young woman in a bar shows a clear barrier to a man sitting next to her. Whether the signal is intentional or unintentional the signal is clear: "I want more space."

Other ways to use one or both arms as a barrier would include the following—but keep in mind that some of these arm movements could just as easily be the most comfortable position for the person at the moment. Always baseline and consider the ancillary body language before concluding the message.

>> Leaning an arm on a table between you and the person next to you.

>> Clutching an arm with the hand of your other arm in front of your body.

>> Placing your folded arms on a table or desk between you and another person.

Sometimes, actions like this are done to send a message deliberately. At other times, they are unintentional, and may be barriering habits begun in your youth.

This next picture shows Tony relaxing in thought waiting for two people to finish a meeting. No barriering, no messaging—just waiting. It is a learned pose that allows him to relax and wait. His eyes have turned to look at the photographer as a result of the camera disturbing his thought. Just moments before, his eyes were engaged down and to his left, as he was deep in contemplation of an issue. The arm cross is his baseline.

ILLUSTRATORS

The arms are often used to illustrate the brain's thoughts. Think back to images of Adolph Hitler's flailing arms driving home his points and whipping people into frenzy.

» Flailing: Animated flailing of the body and arms indicates release of control. Seeing the arms raised above the head in this photo clues you in to the fact that this young woman is letting go. If her arms were held rigidly above her head you would see that as a victory sign in nearly any culture.

» Batoning: Although you know by now that this photo of Kofi is actually a cultural gesture related to eating, it is

exactly the same as an illustrator called batoning—that is, using your arm and hand like a conductor's baton. It is a common action used to drive home a point. A person might use the entire arm, as Hitler did, or simply a pointed finger. In either case he is driving home a point. The more animated, the more intent. Remember his norm when determining animation. Watch for it if someone uses it during a denial, as former President Bill Clinton did in rebuffing the accusation that he had had an affair with a White House intern: In that context, it could well be overcompensation suggesting a lack of honesty.

There are numerous ways the arms can illustrate thoughts, and culture is the primary influence that shapes and inhibits those ways. As you have seen in the example provided by Kofi, a signal does not need to be universally recognizable, because it is you illustrating your thoughts to a specific person or group, and not to the entire

world. (If you're a president or prime minister, gesturing so the "entire world" understands is only one of your challenges.) Most of the time the signaling will occur in time with the words and thoughts when it is genuine and not contrived; the body language supports the words. If you caught a 3-foot fish, your arms would express the length as you get to the climactic moment in the story when you describe the fish. As with Kim's body language here as she explains something, you see hands illustrating her point.

Her hands are in front of her body and even move as if working when she is making her point. As she starts to talk about a person who is in an industry because he loves it and yet cannot see that others are in it for the same reason, her body language clearly illustrates the point of a shift.

Now let's pretend that Kim was telling a story about a fish she caught. I would be suspicious because she has moved the size of the fish illustrator out of her own line of sight.

The number and ways of illustrating with the arms are as numerous as people. How empathically we illustrate is an indicator of the meaning. Elderly people will have a tendency to illustrate with shoulders at lower levels due to physiological changes such as shoulder weakness and loss of muscle, but the illustrators are still evident.

Even though as we age our bodies become decrepit, we still retain enough energy to illustrate, and, although that illustration might not reach the level of our younger counterparts, the level of energy expended is related to the intensity of the feeling.

REGULATORS

Myriad arm movements can be used to regulate conversation.

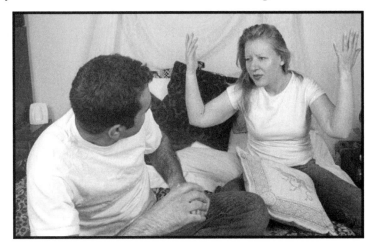

Drooping shoulders and lifeless arms when your partner brings up an old issue to argue about clearly send a regulating signal: "I am tired of discussing this." The body language response is likely an illustrator that tells you "But I'm not! Why don't you get it?"

When combined with open hands, the arms can also signal that someone feels helpless and wants more input from others. Most regulators that are intentional are hand-arm combinations.

Most regulating with the arms comes in the form of sending unintentional signals with the arms that inflame, or soften the conversation.

Examples of regulators include:

>> Bending the arm and holding up the hand like a stop sign.

>> Rotating the arm as if to say "Speed it up."

ADAPTORS

The arms are not often the adaptor itself, but quite frequently coconspirators with the hands, just as in regulating actions. However, people can evolve such bizarre, idiosyncratic adaptors that a person might mill his arms together or rub wrists together to release nervous energy. The most common arms-only adaptors are men swinging arms back and forth in a large circle around their torsos and touching hands in the front or back. Others can include moving the arms in contact with an object when waiting or in high stress; this can be rubbing an arm against a chair or pressing hard with the arm into the torso in an attempt to control nervous energy. Remember that any movement done to release nervous energy so the person feels more comfortable is an adaptor until it becomes a habit. At that point, the idiosyncrasy becomes part of the baseline for the individual.

Hands

If asked to describe your hands without looking at them, you might find that difficult. Not true if I ask you to describe your face. That's ironic, considering you probably look at your hands dozens of times a day and many times more often than you look at your face. Here is the difference: Your hands are tools, and, to some extent, you take them for granted. But in terms of body language, they are nearly as expressive as your face. Remember you also have a tendency to focus on these primary tools when you are stressed. When you gesture, adapt, illustrate, and regulate they are almost always a part of the sentence. Only when you barrier do they occasionally get left out. Even then, your "first tools" are busy at work signaling as you try to contain them.

Review the photos of people with their arms crossed. What do you notice about the hands? There is no universal pattern for what to do with your hands when your arms are crossed. Some leave the hands open and grip the body; others leave them open. Others might ball the fists out of comfort, frustration, or anger. The hands are still trying to communicate when they are trapped by the arms.

Take another example: the fig leaf. Even with the hands stacked at the crotch, because most people talk with hands, they will flex them regardless of where they are.

Hands and arms are partners in illustrating. An orchestration of the two during batoning may involve use of an index finger or all fingers extended, depending on grooming. For example, a person with military experience has been groomed to point with all fingers extended when giving directions. Watch his son or daughter, and you might see the movement repeated if Daddy is a role model for him or her. In that sense, body language is contagious. Try quietly introducing a new illustrator in your next few meetings to verify this. Simply repeat the action in punctuating key statements. Watch for the illustrator to reappear. And note that it may happen when you least expect it.

The hands can play their own part in illustration as well. In places where the trend is toward less demonstrative arms, so the person is forced to contain arms, hands start to speak volumes. The fingers drive home points even if those points are drummed on the biceps of her crossed arms as the person speaks or holds back spoken words and illustrates her thoughts while you speak.

Because arms are primarily transportation devices for the hands, most adaptors are actually conducted by the hands. From rubbing and pulling to petting and stroking, the hands are great tools for releasing nervous energy.

Rubbing temples, massaging the grief muscle, fidgeting hands, picking at cuticles, and finger rubbing are all potentially signs of stress and/or attempts at stress relief. Without knowing the context, however, what you may be observing is nothing more than an annoying personal habit rather than an adaptor.

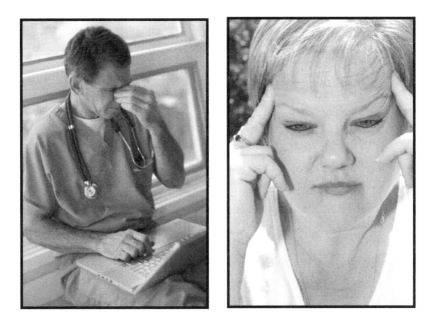

More sophisticated forms of adapting can revolve around containment and channeling energy. If a person is keenly aware of

his "tells" and would prefer not to message, he can easily redirect all of that energy into a single point. I advise anyone who is nervous in front of a crowd to practice channeling energy into the hidden toes or through a point on the fingertip. Jodi does just that in this photo without coaching.

Other less sophisticated examples of trying to control this energy are interlacing fingers, especially in conjunction with tensing other joints of the

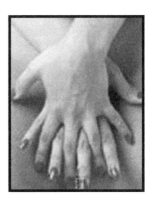

body. The intent is good, but the signaling is more pronounced than allowing the body to do what it naturally would.

Energy level is a good indicator of masking. If a person who normally exhibits high energy, shows little in the way of fidgeting or extraneous movement around stressful situations, she is either well practiced—that is, sophisticated—or not genuinely stressed.

Even the most sophisticated will eventually give in to an adaptor on occasion, whether it is a classic one or an idiosyncratic one. Look closely and you will find it. From picking teeth and nails to nail biting to a soft stoke of the chin, adaptors are the way people release energy. Particularly in a contained environment, hands might be the only body part free to move.

Torso

The three main conditions of the torso, which includes every-thing from the chest to the hips, are rigid, natural, and rounded. A discussion of torso is fundamentally a discussion of posture, because whatever happens at the core—an athlete's term for the torso—dictates whether someone will be slouched, erect, angled, and so on.

Current research suggests that a person's natural state is aroused, and that chemicals in the body put brakes on that state of arousal. So in this discussion, rather than use words like *natural* or *normal,* let's employ the term *neutral* to describe the state falling between conflict and giving up.

When you are in that neutral state, you tend to have posture that reflects your parenting, military training, exercise discipline, and other types of coaching and practice. Your normal posture can also broadcast a good deal about your sense of self-worth and the messages going on in your head, and your relationship with society in general. Think about some very heavy people you have known who feel good about themselves. They don't try to shrink or hide; you feel how comfortable they are with their form. In contrast, think of a normal-sized or slightly overweight person who is constantly dieting and never seems satisfied with how she looks. Often, the posture of these people is like sending up a balloon that reads "I'm not good enough."

This photo captures Kofi reflecting about the fact that his mother recently went through a serious illness that put her in the hospital for while. His torso is rounded, which suggests an emotional state of helplessness, sadness, and related negative feelings of not being in control. A torso in this position conveys almost a lifeless quality. In the course of an interrogation, when a man is about to confess, his body will round, taking on a similarly soft and lifeless posture. It looks as though there is no energy to his limbs. As I mentioned before, the head also droops, so the entire picture is one of a rag doll.

You're only going to go as far in this direction as your operating system will allow, and the same holds true for postures of conflict. If you are physically disciplined, with a naturally erect spine and excellent muscle control, for you to stand sloppy— rounded shoulders, no control over the abdomen—would be awkward. It isn't something you normally do. How far your body would slump, even in a state of depression, would be affected by that. You may curve, but there is a limit to the softness. Even in this relaxed state of walking on the beach with his daughter, this Marine still maintains his clearly defined posture. His hands are not curled into the rigid Marine posture for marching, but his spine still says Marine.

In a state of fight or flight, the torso helps you stand taller and wider than in a neutral state. You want to appear bigger; blood and energy get channeled to your muscles to help make you ready to take action, regardless of whether the action is fighting or running away. It also causes you to put more air into your lungs, which naturally makes your body bigger. Another effect, generally more noticeable on a man, is that your shoulders will square, which forces your palms inward and your fists to grip and your arms to lock. In that position, you're ready to fight, although you still may choose flight.

The body sends unnatural amounts of energy to the joint signal fight or flight, regardless of gender. Women have their own version of the stance I just described, but the basic physiologic responses are the same.

Hips

If a man puts his hands on hips, it means confidence and can be a component of defiance, as long as his fingers are pointed toward his crotch. It is a symbol of masculinity and power, often with feet spread to control more real estate. In contrast, women typically put their hands on their hips with fingers pointed toward the butt cheeks to show the same emotion. If a man does that, it looks feminine. The converse is not true for women. A woman can use either stance and not appear out of the norm.

Contrast the way a man and a women stand to express cockiness or confidence. One demonstrates masculinity by framing the genitals and the other demonstrates feminine power by pointing toward her assets in the rear. Displays of power make us exaggerate the gestures of the gender we identify with. Remember: Once a person has done something enough times it can become part of his baseline, so hands on hips might simply be what he has learned to do with his hands. There are no easy answers.

Women are structurally more predisposed to integrate hip movement into expressions than men are. The hips play a role in a confrontation posture, a submissive posture, and many other behaviors. The hips can be supporting or main components of an illustrator or regulator in women. Putting the hip in motion to angle the body can be a very effective way of conveying an attitude or an order, as in "Don't you dare." Women also commonly use their hips as tools in ways many men wouldn't dream of: closing a car door or resting a baby, for example. A masculine stance dictates that men roll the hips under for less emphasis on the rear end whereas a traditional feminine stance includes pushing the rear end out in a more pronounced and prominent position.

Angling the Body

The way you position the torso in relation to someone can be the defining action in sending a message. So combining a distinct body angle with other movements can change the way those movements are perceived. Bending forward with crossed arms and looking down the bridge of the nose with mouth drawn, or leaning backward and doing the same thing, gives different impressions. It's the difference between threat (the former) and snobbery or skepticism (the latter).

When the arms are crossed, the signal is clear: "Do you think I was born yesterday?" This signaling would be tougher to pick up if it came from a child or young adult. This messaging plays well because of the canvas.

The angle itself can send a message without much other body language as well. Leaning toward or away from another person is a way of using the whole body as a regulator, for example. Without a word or even other bit of body language, the man in this photo sends the signal of disengagement from exhaustion, whether physical or emotional.

On the other hand, in this photo, by leaning and combining the angle with a smirk, this man sends a clear message that he is contemptuous of you.

Someone openly defiant may lean toward you regardless of the expression on his face, but someone being less than openly defiant would lean back slightly. The less control someone feels he has (based on the five factors), the more likely he is to take the approach of the man on the right.

Often, leaning forward can be misunderstood as confrontation or defiance.

With his hands folded and brow indicating uncertainty, his chin is lowered to cover the throat. He is offering his most precious possession (his brain) to you. This is anything but defiance.

Given an opportunity, men will stand at oblique angels as they talk. Most would find it more than uncomfortable to square off face to face. It is a confrontation stance often accompanied by a widely separated foot stance. For most men it feels like a violation of space.

Stature

You can change the way you look in dramatic ways through cosmetic procedures, but your height is currently something that you are stuck with. How you feel about your height can affect your body language in many ways. If you feel short, you may gesture more boldly—that is, away from the torso—than would be considered "usual" or "typical," because you want to occupy more space. Or you may go to extremes in the opposite way—that is, keeping gestures toward the torso—if you think a short person should have "short" movements. Conversely, a very tall man who wants to be perceived as average or a somewhat tall woman who wants to seem petite, may use very constrained gestures. It's very likely a subconscious effort and it is definitely part of the individual's baseline.

Legs

If you've ever watched a dance performance, you've seen the range of expression that a pair of legs can deliver. As with arms, leg movements can serve as illustrators, regulators, adaptors, and barriers.

Illustrators

The legs can work in much the same way as arms to send a message about thoughts. When someone moves her knee to punctuate a thought, it is often missed due to the table or desk used as a barrier.

Legs can send a clear and unambiguous signal, or one or more hidden and unintentional messages. This posed photo is meant to send a clear message about flirtatious sexuality. The intentional messaging in these photos is equally unmistakable. One says "Come here"; the other says, "Approach with caution." Although the message that is sent with this leg cross in the second picture is a

classic barrier, it is being used as an illustrator in this case. Often, using a barrier will result in the opportunity for the legs to become illustrators, as the locked-in-place positioning of the legs creates a prime location for the foot to make the mind's point.

An illustrator could be slight kick, as if making contact with an imaginary football, or crossing the legs for emphasis. Be careful with this one, though. A person's build and training can have a great deal of impact on whether or not the legs are crossed. A man with relatively thick legs will likely often sit with one foot slung over the opposite leg. To some people, that appears cocky, but to the person doing it, that may be the most relaxed way to sit. In contrast, a "European gentleman" would probably sit with legs crossed tightly. A woman can make a deliberate power statement by sitting with her legs crossed and her high heel pointed at someone. It is an illustrator punctuating her confidence through sexuality, confidence through taste in selecting that shoe, and assertiveness by aiming the heel at the person.

BARRIERS

Crossing legs can be a cultural norm or a barrier. If legs are tensed and clenched, it is a barrier; if natural and less rigid, it's likely a cultural adaptation. The posture taken by the man on the previous page is likely an adaptation of leg crossing that fits him. The stance taken by the young woman a barrier showing she feels timid or unsafe. Consider typical barriers used by people every day and where the opportunity to broadcast a punctuation message might occur. In this case, he has created a barrier and is sending intentional messaging with a smirk and a glance over his glasses. Unintentionally, he has created an unnatural stance that will set him up to illustrate even things he does not plan to signal with his hands. He has also created a fantastic platform for telegraphing adaptors. His fingers, exposed foot, and clearly visible other arm have created a signaling theater.

REGULATORS

In the case of the last two: He could easily regulate the conversation by uncrossing his legs and leaning forward or freely swinging the free foot to indicate impatience. Although the young lady next to him is using her barrier for affect, she could easily relax her posture and regulate the conversation by crossing her legs or turning her torso and legs to face you.

In this pose our model is absolutely regulating not only the flow but the content of conversation. Uncrossing her legs would get a different flow to the conversation. Spreading her feet shoulder length apart would evoke another. Though many times this is purely unintentional signaling, this photo definitely shows a young woman in control of her entire body to regulate a conversation.

ADAPTORS

When men, and particularly young men, sit with legs open or crossed, energy can leak from the legs in an adaptor. The adaptors can take the form of feet flailing, or moving the knees back and forth if the legs are apart. Any form of energy release to include milling the legs is possible when a person sits cross-legged, or even when someone stands cross-legged like our model on the previous page.

Feet

Men in general will use feet to increase the amount of space they have. A broad foot stance sends a message of alpha-ness. Oddly enough, the most common time to do this is when someone

is uncertain of his position. After he is the established alpha status, he will find less need for that behavior.

In American culture, and many others, people go to great lengths to hide their feet or at least to disguise their true appearance by adorning them with shoes. Feet are often behind a barrier in addition to the shoes, usually a desk or table, so it's easy to get away with adaptors like curling toes or moving a foot from side to side because no one can see your feet anyway. Other times, you're standing on your feet, so their movement is inhibited. As a result of all of these factors, it's an area of the body that few people think about controlling.

When I teach body language, I select people to come to the front of the room and sit on a table during part of the class. I see some of the same foot action I've seen in real interrogations: As their discomfort grows, their toes point to the door.

One common interpretation of crossing the feet is that the person is trying to shut you out. Don't jump to that conclusion; you need to take context into consideration. Consider his anatomy, first of all. A tall person in a low chair will either have his feet crossed or his knees in his ears. A woman who was raised to adopt "modest" posture will habitually cross her feet because her mother spent 18 years telling her that's how ladies sit.

Sometimes women will also subconsciously turn toes inward, an action that suggests a sense of subjugation, especially in a sexual situation. This submissive pose is common among young women in sexual circumstances in which they are not in charge.

Feet can illustrate, adapt, and barrier. Most often they are not intentionally used as regulators, but can leak that message as well. Think of the foot tapping to adapt, sending a clear message to the other parties that you are ready to leave. The affect is also a regulator, whether you intend it or not. Feet most often serve a supporting role in barriers because it is difficult to protect anything with the feet. The exception is very expensive footwear to project an image of superiority. Feet can stamp, pound, tap, and signal to illustrate along the way—serving again as regulators.

Overall

Head to foot, our whole body is a conduit of communication, some of it intentional and some accidental. As you go about your daily life, look at yourself and those around you, and notice the difference. The five factors of self-awareness, sophistication, grooming, situational awareness, and a sense of others' entitlement continually affect expressions, and they also reflect the influence of previous actions. As you look at what messages others are sending, ask yourself what impact each of the five factors is having on the message.

Just for fun, try to isolate each of the pieces of body language going from head to toes. As you do, label each with the tags: gesture, illustrator, adaptor, barrier, and regulator. For now, think like a child and wonder what that means. We will tie it all up later.

Chapter 6

Scanning the Body: Non-Actions

You would readily associate the topics covered here with the five factors of nurture: self-awareness; sophistication; situational awareness; a sense of others' entitlement and what is proper; and personal style, or grooming. In fact, until you saw in the previous two chapters how movement of body parts reflects them, these may have been the primary aspects of body language that you associate with the factors. They include how you modulate your voice and what you wear, which can be the result of great deliberation or complete thoughtlessness. Another element to consider is the unalterable aspects of your appearance—how you handle what are you and how you perceive others who are different from you.

Distance

Culture plays an important part in how close we stand to each other. Even so, some people just don't seem to have a conventional sense of proximity and are close talkers.

Social distance in many places is around 6 feet—that is, given an option to separate yourself from people you are not involved in conversation with, you will stay 4 to 6 feet from them. When this is violated by necessity, as in an elevator or a crowded street, people disengage and break eye contact. Think of New York City. Though very direct and assertive, few New Yorkers make eye contact on the street. You may think of it as culture, but it is actually very primitive signaling.

In the United States, average conversation distance is about arm's length unless you are very familiar with someone, and then it can be a little closer. When you are intimate with someone, all of that distance disappears. People who are very comfortable with each other and trying to be secretive will often find a reason and way to stand closer.

Vocalics

On June 10, 2009, the English language supposedly got its one-millionth word: *Web 2.0.* Whether or not some of the million have dubious merit, this development is relevant to a discussion of body language for a couple of reasons. First of all, your first language patterns your brain. It's why native English speakers have an inclination to see "anything's possible": You can turn any word into a verb or adjective; you can make an endless number of ugly nouns by adding "ization." Second, we may have a million words, but we still can't always get our point across with words alone. "Would you prefer to lie?" needs tone of voice and emphasis on a word to convey a particular meaning.

Vocalics refers to that kind of vocal communication that affects meaning—pace, pitch, and so on—as well as single syllables like "ah" and "ummm," sharply inhaling, a powerful exhale, humming, and other non-word sounds. You might classify them generally as demonstrative, contained, or normal.

The role they play in communication can vary:

➤ Inserting non-word syllables in a sentence can change the pace of communication. Someone saying "um," for example, interrupts the flow of a sentence in an unintended way. The person may be searching for the right word, so watch for eye movement to see if he's trying to access memory or imagination. Also watch for adaptors. A person relying on those non-word syllables as fillers may just be very nervous.

➤ Depending on what vocal quality you pick up—strident, lyrical, coarse, breathy—you will get a sense of the person's emotions. When someone explosively exhales while you're talking, you have probably triggered either strong disbelief or frustration. A sharp inhale could be an indication of fear or surprise. Watch what the brow and mouth do at the same time to narrow down the possibilities.

You may also pick up utterances that capture a tone or pronunciation that seems abnormal to you. Such subtle aspects of speech can give away information about where a person grew up or the kind of people he has spent a lot of time with. If you pick that up, you have an extra clue about cultural influences: If the person lived in that area or with people from that area long enough to pick up such a regionalism, then chances are good that the body language shows it, too. You can tell a Southerner by the shape of the mouth, and when non-Southerners try to mimic the accent, they have to reshape their mouths to be convincing. CNN's Campbell Brown and actress Holly Hunter are two great examples of women you can identify as Southern even with the sound off. We Southerners have a tendency to speak in flat vowels; we don't round our mouths, and that leads to a flatter mouth.

I have an Indian associate with a unique accent. He has developed a high-pitched voice that effectively disguises where he is from. The mechanics of it involves lifting his tongue higher in his mouth. Interestingly, he has also adjusted certain aspects of his body language to "Americanize" them because he realizes that some of his native gestures (described briefly in Chapter 3) might inhibit his communication with non-Indians.

Most people who have experienced vocalic shifts are not nearly as aware as the Indian gentleman. Maryann had a friend who spent years teaching English as a foreign language in Japan. When he came back to the United States, she noticed a distinct change in the pitch of his voice. He had begun speaking Japanese when he was abroad, and apparently, as he adopted the tones of the language instead of just learning vocabulary; it changed the way he sounded in English.

Clothing, Emblems, and Other Add-Ons

A badge, a piece of clothing, a watch—all of these need to be grouped with movements and sounds as part of body language in many cases. They fall into two categories: those intentionally worn to send a message, and those worn for personal significance.

Like a gesture from a culture foreign to yours, a piece of clothing or accessory means nothing to the uninitiated, or to people who simply don't care. A middle-aged man came in to a job interview with a very expensive watch, cufflinks, and pin that all signified he belonged to an exclusive fraternity. Because his membership in it had no bearing on his qualifications for the job, the interviewer ignored the bling. That made the man uncomfortable; clearly, the interviewer's opinion of him would rise if only he'd noticed them. And so the candidate gently hiked up the sleeve of his coat to show off the cufflinks and watch, and lightly touched the pin. That didn't elicit a comment either, so he just blurted out that he was a member of the fraternity. During the interview, his agitation gave rise to adaptors. And his sense of self-worth, which in a literal way he was wearing on his sleeves, was obviously not shared by the interviewer; that fact, too, contributed to his need for adaptors. The poor guy was a fidgeting mess.

Comedian Jimmy Fallon, now host of *Late Night With Jimmy Fallon*, tells a story of his first appearance on a TV talk show. His nervousness about being a guest on the *Late Show with David Letterman* drove him to get fashion advice from a stylist who dressed Fallon in a $300 T-shirt and $200 jeans. The first thing Letterman said to him was something like "Thanks for dressing up." Instead of the T-shirt becoming part of the body language of "stylish, hip" Jimmy Fallon, Letterman's remark convinced all but the most discerning fashionistas that he was a grungy comedian who didn't care enough to dress up for the show. Fallon's fashion statement lost its power, just as the job candidate's did.

Other the other hand, selection of clothing or emblems may be part of a message that isn't obvious. Many people thought my friend's father was a snob because he wore his Phi Beta Kappa key on his suit every day. It served as a personal reminder of his standards; it was like he was telling the world: "Hold me accountable because this is what I'm capable of." Those kinds of personal emblems, whether they are religious symbols, awards, or a piece of jewelry from someone who means a lot, can be a powerful symbol of personal standards and a daily motivator. Assuming you know the meaning of someone else's emblem without having it explained is just as bad as drawing a conclusion about crossed arms when you know nothing about the person's baseline, context, or culture.

If you've ever heard someone say "That person thinks he's better than I am" after taking one look at a person, that remark signals major insecurity. My response is: "How could you possibly know that just by looking at someone?" It's the same as people assuming that my friend's father wearing a Phi Beta Kappa key is a gesture aimed at the world, instead of what it really means.

I noticed something interesting as the economic downturn in the United States forced many unemployed, well-qualified people to face the fact that good jobs were scarce: Many people I encountered in airports during my frequent travels had made changes in their body language to try and overcome the bad odds. I wanted to make sure I wasn't imagining the change, so I located articles covering that very topic. Many business travelers no longer thought "business casual" should be their default dress when they flew; they started wearing suits. They did not want to be recognized as slackers. From their confident strides to their silk ties, they wanted to be seen as successful. It reminds me of the old adage of trying to outrun the bear: You don't have to outrun the bear; you just have to outrun your friend.

Disabilities and Differences

A wandering eye, shaking from Parkinson's disease, a collapsed torso from an accident—these are many of the factors that can become part of someone's baseline. In reading the individual's body language, those factors are not types of messaging in themselves; they have a place in repertoire of the person's normal, relaxed body language.

With disability comes an adaptation of human behavior; it is not dissimilar from adapting to a new culture. Communication may take on forms considered atypical or abnormal by society.

A birth defect may place someone in a lifelong effort to move toward more "normal" body language. And when the disability occurs in adult life through trauma or disease, the person may suddenly feel compelled to readjust all kinds of body language to fit in. The individual's baseline—that is, what is normal for that person, or what becomes normal for that person once she adjusts to her new circumstances—may involve expressions and gestures that seem foreign to you. Pay attention to patterns of behavior and watch for deviations as you would with anyone else.

People who are a different color, size, or shape from others around them may also try to adapt through body language. Others will go the other extreme and emphasize their difference. Again, both patterns can become part of the individual's baseline. I have a very large friend who stands more than 6 feet tall and weighs about 350 pounds. He looks like he could pound you into the ground, and he uses that to his advantage. I've been in a truck with him when another guy was edging too close to him in traffic. He said to me, "Watch this" and began throwing his arms around as though he were in a rage. The other guy backed off. He made a conscious decision to use the body language of very big man and learned to use it with great effect, making the "little people" around him feel even smaller. In this case, he was intentionally signaling something other than he was thinking, but with intent. It worked because even the dimmest of us can recognize rage, and, on someone that size, it is powerful.

Chapter 7

Tying It All Together

L ike most anything else, body language analysis can be overdone. To suggest that every action a person takes has meaning would be insulting to your intelligence and less than correct. Study body language as clusters of symptoms. If it looks like he is sitting on a tack as he controls his hands, there is nervous energy trying to leave him. His other indicators can help you to understand why he is a bundle of nerves. If he really is sitting on a tack, you will see a spectrum of pain-related moves rather than anxiety-based. Most of this is simple observation.

Expertise is about knowledge intersecting people. No amount of my study of people can replace the intimate knowledge you have of someone. Interrogators analyze behavioral symptoms. This helps us to understand drives and motivation, and to create a situation ideal for cooperation. All of that is overlain onto a tremendous amount of knowledge-gathering and study of our target.

If you think you can learn a snippet here and a snippet there to quickly analyze everyone and anyone you meet, you have missed the key point thus far.

Common Mistakes

Throughout the book, you have seen reasons why it's easy to misinterpret body language. In this section, I want to spotlight a few traps you could fall into specifically, because you now have an increased awareness of both intentional and unintentional messaging. In other words, now that you have accumulated some understanding of body language, it's easy for you to go around reading meaning into everything.

Scratching

Whether it involves the nose, leg, arm, or ear, scratching is almost always a natural response to stimulus, unless it is habitual and idiosyncratic behavior. That is not to say the stimulus cannot be stress, and the cause something other than a real itch. As you watch a person, realize a scratch can be a response to an insect bite, a rash, or some other reaction. More importantly, a scratch can be a natural response to stress-induced itching, too. When people become hypersensitive as a result of stress, things itch, and sometimes the person scratches his skin simply because it's a default action.

Posture and Torso

People naturally have demeanor that is controlled or slouchy, or, as with most people, somewhere in between. To assume, without any background information, that sloppy posture means anything other than sloppy posture is projection on your part. To assume rigid, straight-neck posture automatically sends a particular message is more of the same. With no knowledge of the person's past experiences or grooming, you cannot deduce something about his mental state.

Like an interrogator who has observed a subject before any interaction, you often have some knowledge of people before meeting them for the first time. If you don't, and are assessing a person you just met, suspend judgment and pay attention to what the person does normally as you speak. Notice her approach to interaction, and compare the interaction with you to her exchanges with another person or group. If she responds freely, comfortably, and relaxed in a given group and then turns into a robotic, rigid, traffic-directing cop in the next group, it indicates her perception of self-identify with that group. Similarly, if she is natural in a given group and then looks rounded and conciliatory in the next group, her understanding of her position is less than alpha for the second group. To really understand where she fits, though, you need to watch the dance between her and others. It is entirely possible that she is a master of body language and the soft self-deprecating act is simply to make others more comfortable because they are not comfortable with the traffic cop in the room. Finally, a person who moves absolutely with ease from group to group without changing his demeanor or mannerisms is equally comfortable in all groups.

Signs of Anxiety

With some people, you may observe a growing agitation during the course of a meeting or long conversation. Don't necessarily think it's you. The person may be a smoker waiting for a lull to excuse himself or someone who's hungry or suddenly remembers that her kid needs to be picked up from school. Create the lull that gives the individual a chance to take the action required to alleviate the anxiety.

If a person you've just met is fidgety, keep watching to see if it's part of the baseline. Some people seem to move all the time, especially one foot, as though some up-tempo music is playing inside the person's head. If it looks as though the music has suddenly stopped, then wonder why. You may have just said or done something to engage the individual so completely—in a good or bad way—that you have caused a deviation from baseline.

I recently had an experience with a very anxious person that reminded me that interpreting body language is a matter of reading symptoms; it's not a tool for mind reading. I was interviewing three top candidates for a position. One of the candidates walked in with an "oh, dammit" look on his face. It was impossible to miss, and I asked him what the problem was. He said, "I was hoping you weren't the guy." He explained that he'd been told a Greg Hartley would interview him for the position, and searched for information online with the name. He found a reference to the fact that, in one of my previous books, I had told a story about conducting interviews. That led him to other searches and the discovery of my background as an interrogator and body language expert. His frank admission that those facts shook him made it easy for us to move forward with the interview. Had he not admitted to knowing anything about me, it could have cost him any further consideration for the job. I would not have known why he appeared to be anxious and cranky. All I could do was notice the symptoms that he was extremely uncomfortable.

Common Wisdom

The four pieces of guidance I offer here to help you avert common mistakes are these:

1. Communication is negotiation.

2. You may not be able to identify the emotion being expressed, but you should be able to tell if it's positive or negative.

3. Body language analysis is not ESP.

4. Substances that affect the mind and body affect body language.

Negotiation

In the Army's language school, I learned Arabic for the purpose of asking questions and gaining information. Even though all language might be called "negotiation language," because it is supposed to help us come to a common understanding, my training specifically emphasized that role. Using Arabic in real situations, I would often hit a situation in which I needed to negotiate toward a common meaning by using whatever words I happened to know. And like anyone else who finds himself in a situation where vocabulary fails, I resorted to gesturing to help get my point across.

One day, I needed a pipe wrench, a pair of pliers, and some electrical tape. Oddly enough, those phrases had never come up in the political discussions we had in language school. So I walked up to a guy who was doing some handy work and said, "I need some tools." He asked me what kind. "I need a thing that turns two pipes together" is roughly what I said as I used my hands to illustrate what I wanted. His eyes got big and he muttered that he understood what I wanted, used the word for pliers, and then gave me the tool I needed. If he hadn't understood, and maybe brought me something completely different, we would have gone back to negotiating.

Take it a step further. What if we'd had no common spoken language? I start using my hands to illustrate a twisting motion, and suggest an opening that gets larger and then smaller. What is he supposed to think I want? Depending on this local culture, he might think I'm asking for a smoke, something sexual, or any one of a number of things.

Keep negotiation in mind whenever you try to understand someone's body language (or spoken language). Work with the individual in the spirit of cooperation and compromise, not "x means this, no matter what you're really trying to express."

Positive and Negative Emotions

Typically, when people express positive emotion, they don't constrain the expression, but sometimes they feel they have to because of the context. In a compromising position, people tend not to blurt out what they're thinking in word or in deed. Yet the thoughts and accompanying emotions are still there, and they will bleed out in unintended ways. Instead of illustrators adamantly punctuating points, adaptors will creep into the conversation. You see that occurring in negative situations or in containment of a positive situation.

You see this kind of expression at lot at funerals where people in attendance truly loved the individual. They want to express the joy they associate with him, but feel it's inappropriate because of the solemnity of the occasion, so they hold back. The result can include fidgeting, shifting, and behavior that's odd for those people. The emotions have to bleed somehow. They contain their personalities to the point at which their behavior and conversation become unnatural for them.

Every day, people do that in meetings, on dates, and in other situations where they feel compromised. As the other person who is trying to read the body language, you need to know that, just because someone is bleeding emotion through adaptors, that does not mean it's not a positive experience for them.

Negative emotion on the other hand is something that people generally go to great lengths to contain. Rage, grief, disappointment, and others in the family of negative feelings have a way of surfacing, often because elements of facial action don't come together to create a coherent expression. A jaw set in rage trumps the smile on the face.

Forget ESP

Body language analysis is not mindreading.

In doing a project for the Discovery Channel, one of the producers asked me to watch a video of someone committing suicide. His question: "How could you tell what he was going to do?" My answer: "I couldn't. I read body language, not minds." A person considering personal extinction has a lot happening concurrently, both mentally and emotionally, and if I could sort through all that internal noise, I would have God-like powers. It reminds me of the dilemma our intelligence services faced when the United States tried to determine whether or not Saddam Hussein would invade Kuwait. He lined up his troops and armaments, but, because he didn't even trust his closest advisors enough to level with them all the time, the only person who knew whether Saddam would invade was Saddam.

You can know a person inside and out and still get surprised. You can rarely look at a person and know what he's thinking; you can only see symptoms that he's having an emotional issue, contemplating, and recalling. Knowing what is really going on inside his head takes powers beyond body language analysis.

In exercises demonstrating body language, I can appear to have that skill, however. The way I direct people can force them into single-sensory channel. I ask a specific question that provokes a particular, predictable type of eye movement. When I do this on the radio, it probably does seem to some listeners as though I can read people's minds and foresee their behavior.

But real life doesn't consist of straightforward questions and single-sensory experiences. Stimulation from multiple sources has us listening to conversations, other people's phone calls, television, and street noise all at the same time. We may be looking at someone's face, but can't keep our eyes from wandering toward the person who just walked through a door, as well as the action on the TV screen behind him.

Just keep your eyes on the symptoms and don't convince yourself you are actually inside someone else's head.

The Impact of Substances

If you decide to exercise your new skills at a party, think again. As I keep saying, getting a baseline on someone is essential to your understanding of her signals, and, if those signals are being distorted by something, you may be off on the person's baseline.

I once worked with a cinematographer who interned under Jerry Springer and asked him how much of the seemingly spontaneous rage that occurred on camera was staged. People brought in to confront each other are kept offstage in rooms that are painted bright colors and are only allowed to drink caffeinated beverages.

Stimulants and depressants affect your body language because they affect the degree of tension in your muscles, ability to focus, reaction time, and other aspects of movement. To whatever extent they could, the people who "prepared" guests on the Jerry Springer show supported the body language of raucous behavior. Many a host has done the same thing at a party.

Basic Rules for the Real World

One key element always plays into the analysis of anyone in an interrogation—that is, the artificiality of the situation. When we interrogate, no person will come at us full bore with expressions of anger, defiance, and rage. In fact, there is an effort to mute all body language. Oddly enough, this same phenomenon is true in every situation: All but a few of us have masters of some sort. Whether we mute body language out of social norms or because of the preferences of a boss, something prevents us from full expression of our thoughts. Add to that the fact most us do not want to be that transparent and you find that you need to learn to read subtleties, not full-blown demonstrations.

Think for just a minute about a 2-year-old toddler showing defiance. The 2-year-old has little in the way of self-awareness, and in fact the self-awareness he does have is a detriment instead of a benefit. His understanding of human interactional norms is limited to what has been imparted to him through nurture, and even that has been filtered through the mind of a 2-year-old. Arguably, a parent has driven some level of self-control into him, albeit limited. He is oblivious to situation and entitlements of others. His favorite word is *mine*. In defiance, his face is probably contorted into a sneer, with his chin up, eyes ablaze, and jaw set. In this early stage of life, his lips are likely even pushed forward to exaggerate the jaw thrusting forward. He might place his hands on hips to send a clear message that the only entitlement that matters is the one you have overlooked: his. His body language is rigid, shouting displeasure; his hands or feet pound to illustrate his point. His eyes narrow to focus more clearly on you or the other offender. His voice is raised to explain his point to you and his face might be flush with anger. He uses his favorite word as explicitly as possible in telling you that the remote is no longer yours: *mine!* When you do not appear to understand, he enunciates more clearly. This is the full-blown state of defiance for the child. As he ages, the expressions will change, in part due to his understanding of his place in life. But even as it changes, his defiance will retain remnants of this early messaging because when he was 2 years old, the demonstration worked. Maybe it didn't work every time, but often enough to get his point across and to create a usable form of communication.

So by the time he is 8 or 9, he no longer does all of that. Instead, he does this:

Human emotion will dictate how body language displays itself. Instead of referring to emotions in the upcoming run-down of basic rules of interpretation, however, I call them behaviors because we are concerned with outcomes, not internal process. Reading body language does not guarantee you can understand exactly which piece of stimulus caused the effect. As a practitioner you are more concerned with the effect.

Basic Rules

1. Some imaging is intentional; some is not. Like the alpha chimp, if a person intends to send the message of intimidation, he might simply broadcast a set of signals that are a packaged unit. This would probably involve dropping eyebrows to create a ledge and setting his jaw as he looks at you, squaring shoulders, and leaning forward to send a message while filling his lungs with air and balling his fists. This is a package of behaviors he has used throughout his life to signal that he is displeased, and it has worked; the package has become a tool much like words for this person. So although it is not a checklist, he consciously thinks through it. It is intentional messaging.

2. Intentional messaging is tempered by threat. Just as messaging in the primate world is controlled by danger to self, humans control messages delivered in word or deed based on the message receiver. When you watch animals of any kind, the pecking order comes into play. A young dog will bully other young dogs with boisterous body language and aggression; the same is true for primates, lions, and all other social animals. These dominance games are the politics of the animal kingdom. The minute an alpha or other higher-up in the pecking order arrives, this boisterous body language of dominance becomes more rounded and softened. In most animals the body language shifts to one of downright submission. On occasion, this body language will

still leak bits of contempt until the dominant establishes control. The same is true with humans. If you walk to the water cooler and hear Eddie Haskell spout his bravado with the boys it will only last until the boss shows up. Then the other side of Eddie will come out: the supplicant side that wants approval from the alpha. It is the duplicitous nature of humanity. Each of us instinctively knows when to filter our body language and show deference. The problem is, unlike a leopard or hyena, we have a frontal cortex that runs other programs while we are trying to message submission. So although we are trying to send that message of soft white underbelly deference, our internal voice is also messaging. This unintentional messaging is often as meaningful as what we are intentionally sending.

3. Intensity can override filter. Sometimes, no matter how we try to signal deference to the boss, the emotion we are feeling is just too intense to allow us to defer. Filtering our messaging is a cognitive skill. We think through whether something is appropriate before we say or do it. When a primary emotion like anger or fear becomes so intense that it consumes the mind, it is difficult to control the messaging. Human brains have evolved through the stages of reptilian-mammalian-primate to give us an operating system that is designed for cognitive thought, emotional response, or simply surviving. Stimuli can turn off layers of our brains and take away the capability to use these layers. Intense, primary emotions like anger and fear often turn off the primate brain and cause us to use the mammalian brain reacting instead of thinking. These primary emotions carry inborn signaling recognizable at a distance for other humans. This is the universal body language covered in Chapter 2. Though this might not rise to the level of fist-pounding and snarling of teeth, the rage associated with anger can cause us to lose control of all but the most intentional messaging.

4. The five factors affect all rules. Each of the five factors impacts how we respond in messaging. The more self-aware a person is, the more conscious of signals he becomes. Even people who have no idea of the meaning of body language struggle with what to do with hands in an awkward situation. It requires a level of self-awareness to understand that the hands are doing something to begin with. Oddly enough, a little knowledge can often make us more keenly self-aware without a true understanding of what the signals mean; I refer you to the arm-crossing discussion. Once our subject understands he is doing something, the next question is: "How much sophistication does he have?" This sophistication is two-pronged: What is his place in the grand scheme, and what does a given signal mean? Perhaps he is keenly aware that he is subordinate to you, but unaware that his hands in front of his crotch signal insecurity. Assuming the fig-leaf position therefore shows self-awareness without much sophistication. Grooming can sometimes play a significant role in the same way that, once in a while, a blind squirrel finds a nut.

This is the case for a person who has been taught through years of grooming to keep his hands still as much as possible. Although he might have no clue about where he fits in the hierarchy, might not be self-aware, and might not understand anything about body language, he defaults to instructions programmed into him sometime in his past. Perhaps Sister Mary Katherine taught him to sit with his hands folded until called on, and that lesson serves him well. If he is displaced, however—essentially a stranger in a strange land—even the good Sister's attempts to help him act appropriately in any situation will be fruitless. In a culture with different sets of signals, his lack of movement could be misperceived. And if a person truly understands where he fits and what his body language all means, and he is among his peers, the sense of what is proper deference to others' rights will trump all other signals. The exception is someone who is truly out of control. So, for instance, while you might be demanding of a superior, your sense of propriety will likely signal insecurity about the demand. But if your superior arouses a strong sense of indignity through an insult, then, even though you know what's appropriate, you may release the brakes on your behavior.

5. Distinguish between intentional and unintentional messaging. Typically, people demonstrate their thoughts with illustrators, regulators, and gestures. Regulators are attempts to control the conversation, and illustrators, attempts to clarify point. All can creep in unintentionally, but they are often deliberate tools of communication. Barriers and adaptors are intended to give more space and comfort to the person using them. They are most often unintentional unless the person using them is keenly aware of their messaging. Just remember that sometimes an arm cross is just an arm cross. Baselining is essential.

As you go about applying body language analysis, remember this is an evolving skill. You can take the basics here and work your way to a new level of understanding. I am no magician; I am a practitioner. This book is intended to make you an apprentice. Learning is a cycle. You are going to miss it sometimes—we all do. Relax and practice. Trust no gimmicks and keep your eyes open.

Chapter 8

Your Changing Body Language

Global and personal influences will continue to have an effect on your body language and that of people around you. Societal trends and technology—two intertwined influences—and your developing skills in analyzing other people's body language will somehow impact how you move, how you express yourself through clothing and other emblems, and what utterances are appropriate for the occasion.

Changing Times

Through the ages, the definition of "normal" body language has changed dramatically. Looking at photos, movies, and television through the ages will give you a clear sense of how body language has changed.

In early photos, the pinhole camera forced people to into posed position; they had to be prepared for the camera, and probably many people holding dead-still for photos had no idea what the end result would look like. The photo on the following page, taken

around 1888, shows a typical result. People in photos of the time looked either filled with pride or angry—pride because they could afford to get the photograph taken, or angry because they had to sit still for so long. You would have a hard time capturing the body language of surprise, embarrassment, excitement, or any sudden emotion. Now, with high-speed digital photography, photos can be candid, as you can see in the next picture. You can spontaneously record genuinely expressive body language.

If you watch a movie today that you saw and liked 20 years ago, certain things might seem odd about it. Not only do movie-making techniques evolve, but the way people express emotions and regional dialect in a movie can also evolve. The way people in movies telegraphed their role—good guy or bad guy—has changed, too. Often, you could spot the villain because he shuffled around, whereas the good guy stood up straight. In the post-war 1940s, the tailored clothing and near-rigidity of the way both men and women walked reflected the strong influence the military had on many aspects of American life.

Some pieces of body language that are common now didn't exist a few decades ago. People walk down the street ostensibly talking to themselves all the time now. Doing that used to mean a person was crazy; now it means she's on a phone call. This is one of many ways trends and technology have affected body language.

Multitasking

Another way technology has prompted changes is in our attempts to multitask.

Fortunately, humans have done a good job of inventing machines that multitask to make up for the fact that our brains are not designed to do it. Sources of research substantiating this assertion are as diverse as the Federal Aviation Administration's pilot training program, a 2002 University of Rhode Island study, and your elementary school teacher who gave you the challenge of patting your head while you rub your belly.

The fact that people have so many gadgets going simultaneously that multitasking is part of everyday life has an interesting effect on body language. People either don't perceive a stimulus and therefore don't respond to it—the so-called tunnel vision effect studied in the University of Rhode Island research I referenced—or they overreact because their brain wasn't able to process the relative importance of the stimulus. For example, a driver who is fooling with the GPS system jerks the steering wheel and slams on the brake in an over-response to a bicyclist coming up alongside the car.

In less dangerous situations, such as a date where both people are juggling phone calls and text messages with their own human interaction, normal responses will be affected by the multitasking. A calm moment walking down the street can instantly shift to an emotionally charged one, with arms flailing or adaptors kicking in depending on what the text message said. How is the person who didn't get the upsetting text message supposed to read and respond to the flailer?

Changing Skills

As you develop your skills of body language analysis, you may likely notice and cultivate changes in your own body language that are even more dramatic than those related to societal trends and technology. The reason is that the five factors will start to change for you and so you can expect some changes in the way you intentionally use body language. Your self-awareness, sophistication, situational awareness, sense of others' entitlements, and even your grooming will probably move up a notch.

Consider two opposites on the spectrum of knowing how to use body language proactively. After that, refer back to the insights on illustrators, regulators, barriers, and adaptors to assess where you sit on the spectrum, as well as where others around you sit.

The character Miranda Priestly in *The Devil Wears Prada* wields tremendous power at her magazine, but the intimidation she perpetrates emanates more from her thorough control over herself than it does from her control over the business. She has learned that a set jaw and a whisper can command more attention than a rant— although she's perfectly capable of a rant as well.

In contrast, I was once coaching a young man who was a pushover. From his cherubic face to his chubby body to his soft demeanor, he came across as a self-deprecating loser. He was working with me so he could learn to stand up to the bullies in his everyday business life. I played the bully in our session, saying in a direct, quiet tone with my eyes narrow until they were slits: "Does your company screen for low intelligence, or did they just get lucky?" If I had shouted or put an edge of sarcasm in my voice, it would have been less abusive than simply saying it. I spoke harshly in a way that violated his entitlement. I drove the point home in a way that was even worse than if I'd been out of control, which would have suggested emotion rather than judgment.

Before this young man consciously integrated the body language of a confident, competent person, he looked lifeless—a look I've seen many times in the course of an interrogation. Even fidgeting and twitching are signs of mental and physical activity, but someone who goes limp shows no power whatsoever. He is a defeated individual.

If you are closer to the self-deprecating young man than you are to Miranda Priestly—and that would be the case for most of humanity, I think—then refer to the information in this handbook to help yourself use body language as well as read others' signals. If you see someone else doing something you find annoying or weak, ask yourself if and when *you* do it.

} *Chapter 9* {

Case Studies

Body language has great similarities to other forms of human communication. Imagine trying to learn a foreign language and understanding only a dozen words after several lessons—and they are the easy ones, not necessarily the ones you will need. As you apply your new skills in body language, consider that you have grasped the equivalent of prepositions and articles. You would not do well in conversation understanding only *from*, *to*, and *the*. With practice and with exposure to these new words in context, your dozen words multiply, and, at some point, you comprehend whole sentences and paragraphs.

As you learn body language, it's okay to grasp isolated concepts— like individual words—and look at what each of these pieces really means. This foundation is essential, enabling you to get to a point of not needing to think about rudimentary elements, and instead to focus on both hidden and intentional messages. But like the 12-word interpreter, you can make dramatic mistakes by not linking all of the elements of body language to create a true understanding of what is being communicated.

Pull it all together—that's what the case studies in this chapter help you to do. Look at each of the two photos before reading the text, and make notes about you think is going on. Can you assess emotions? Focus? Relationships? What role do certain objects a person is wearing or holding have in creating a barrier or adapting to a situation? You could even make a game out of this. Have a couple of your friends read the book at the same time you do and then get together with a couple of friends who haven't read it. See what you and the other newly minted body language "experts" spot versus those who rely on preconceived notions related to culture and instinct.

As a final recommendation, set up your own case studies. Pay attention to photos or to video with no sound that are associated with some news story or pop culture event. Make your assessment of what people are communicating with their body language first, and then find out the real story afterward. In time and with practice, you should see improvement and you will have cultivated an invaluable skill.

Case Study 1: Waiting for a Train

This basic photo gives you an opportunity to see body language with minimal interaction and passive stimulus. Whether in Tokyo, London, or New York, the premise is still the same: These individuals are moving through a tunnel waiting for the next train. The advantage of this photo is that it simplifies looking at snippets of body language separated from social interaction.

Whether traveling alone or accompanied, with few exceptions, each of these people is not engaged with another person, although more than one is focused on another person.

» *The older woman on the far left* has her attention on someone, and it appears to be the young woman in the skirt with the bags. The older woman is clearly interested in the people on the platform as she vigilantly awaits her turn to get on the train. You would describe it that way because she is standing across the white line. But she is focused on others because, if she were interested only in the train, she would look straight ahead as those in the center of the photo are doing. Her posture is relaxed and natural for her. She has probably adopted this posture over the years. She holds her bag in a comfortable position, and is alert and in control of it, but neither anxious nor apprehensive. Although you cannot see her face well it is clear she is in data-intake mode: interested and focused without engagement.

» *The young woman to her right* in the skirt might be barriering subconsciously, but more than likely is holding the bag in front of her to share the load between her arms. Look for the rounding of her shoulders, even under the leather jacket, that indicates load bearing. She is looking slightly up and to her right. Did something catch her eye or is she imagining how fabulous she is going to look in whatever is in the bag? Her focus is internal, and she is not engaged.

» *Next to her in a very dark outfit* is another young woman almost fully obscured from our sight. We can see a bit of her face as she appears to be focused on the arriving train.

» *The woman with a child* is focused on the train, ready to go, and with one purpose: get moving. She stands firmly on her heels, but her body is tensed and ready to move. Along with the blurring of the moving train arriving in this photo, also notice the woman's head is moving to focus on the incoming train. The little girl seems preoccupied with the feet of the young man at the very front of the group. It could well be that only her mother's admonition prevents her from engaging him with "what big feet you have!" She carries the ultimate childhood barrier: a doll or stuffed animal—the equivalent of Linus's ever-present blanket. Both mobile barrier and object of adapting, it is a powerful security tool. Will she outgrow it, or simply find a substitute?

» *The young man in the very back with the baggy jeans* stands as most young men do: feet about shoulder-width apart. His arms are in front of him, holding some sort of object as he barriers his torso. He is focused and might wish engagement with the object of his focus, the fully obscured young woman to the front. He is obviously traveling with the older man with the cloth on his head to his right. We can only guess at the relationship, but know that they are close due to the proximity with which they stand on this less-than-crowded platform; this closeness indicates comfort and trust. Usually this degree of nearness indicates a familial bond.

» *The man with the cloth on his head* stands with his feet close together. It could either be a stance he has become accustomed to or one dictated by biology. His left hand is active, and, although we cannot tell exactly what he is doing, this could indicate adapting. It is not reaching for his wallet, because that is clearly on the opposite hip. Is he putting something he was using away in preparation for the train, or recovering something he will need? His head tilts to indicate he is involved with an internal conversation of some type, but without seeing his face, it is not possible to tell whether it is a logical discussion or an emotional issue. His focus seems internal, and he is not engaged.

» *In front and center, almost totally obscured, are two young men.* The one on the left spreads his feet and legs well beyond shoulder width, almost to an exaggerated point. Is he trying to claim turf because he feels uncomfortable, or just standing comfortably? Either way, it is a learned behavior and results from his past. The young man standing next to him in the baseball cap does not appear to be barriering at all, and his head appears to be tilted down. He could be lost in thought and therefore showing a loss of situational awareness. He stands closer to the tall man than he does to anyone else, which could indicate either they are traveling together or that he is socially oblivious. The distance is not so close as to indicate a familial bond, but the distinct nature of young male relationships in American culture means even standing close will be mitigated. He will stand closer to a young male friend than a stranger, but not much.

» *In terms of situation awareness the young woman to the hard right* of the photo is oblivious. Based on the natural stance of the other two women in the photos with total control of their purses, this woman look like a poster girl for bag snatching. She may well be a tourist in the big city. At the very least, she has a different understanding of the landscape from the other women. She appears to be engaged with someone on her right and in conversation.

» *The man in the jean jacket* has one purpose: to get on the train. Like the older woman on the left, he is across the white line, but facing forward, focused, and ready to board. Notice his hands are in a pseudo hip-grasp; he has his hands to the rear and yet does not appear feminine at all. This is a typical masculine pose and variant of hands on hips.

» *The man to his right* is focused on the train with his hands in pockets. The style of clothing he wears suggests that this is his norm. If he is milling his fingers in those pockets or counting change, we would know he is less comfortable than he appears here.

All of this is body language with passive stimulus! Most of the action is going on in the heads of our subjects and quietly leaking out of the body. This is simple observation of a snapshot in time and has no baseline. More importantly, most of the people are dancing solo. Next, let's look at what happens when we add interaction.

Case Study 2: Waiting for an Interview

Before you start reading, take a five-second glance and decide for yourself what is going on in this photo.

In this open-call interview, people are waiting to meet with the men at the desk—waiting to sit in the leather-covered chair across from the decision-makers. Each of the people in the line is waiting for his or her turn. Each has a unique body language response to the stimulus. The chair creates a tangible input for stress.

In this case study, I will present you with an analysis of behavioral symptoms frozen in time with no knowledge of the personalities of the participants. By its nature, this is a combination of absolutes and observations. To get a more accurate picture, I would need to know these people and see how events transpired.

>> Focus on the young man on the right in the checked shirt and the young woman with her hair pulled up.

  >> **Him:** Either he is not there for the interview or he missed the dress code. He is uncomfortable with the situation and, in this case, the arms are barriers to give him more space. His fists are tightly balled behind his arms. Oddly enough, he is faced away from the three men interviewing. Although his discomfort could be from his attire, or from the interviewers, it is more likely caused by the person he is facing. Something is probably going on between him and the young woman causing him to barrier; all of the rest are just add-ons. His base comfort level with the young woman is evident: He is faced directly toward her and closer than normal. His head is leaned forward; all of his focus and engagement are clearly on her. Notice that although he feels comfortable enough with her to get this close, his general discomfort is causing him to barrier, but that action is useless in blocking out the gaze of the interviewers. It would also be overkill, because he has turned his back on them—the

ultimate barrier. He is leaned in, suggesting he is speaking in language intended for her only, and appears to be in physical contact with her (upper right of the photo). His body language says he is not eager to go into an interview, or at least not this one. It's likely he is here for another purpose.

>> **Her:** In part to get her ear closer to him, her head is tilted slightly down and to the right (your right). She clenches her bag as if it is trying to escape from her body. She is slightly bent forward at the shoulders, which might be her normal posture, but has weight on her front foot, which is clearly pointed away from her current conversation and toward the interview chair. She appears ready and interested in the interview process; her focus, posture, and grasp on the bag make her appear eager to get to the chair. Whether her keenness to get to the chair is to escape the stimulus of the young man or just to get to the interview is a tough call.

>> Focus on the two women to the immediate left of the pair just discussed.

>> The women are having a private conversation in public. Both show signs of trying to communicate without the world hearing.

>> The brunette is using her portfolio as an immense barrier, holding on tightly to suggest she needs more space. Her stance puts her at a 180-degree angle to the rest of the applicants, and she is mostly hidden from the interviewers by the group in front of her. What view is left, she covers with her portfolio or hand. In shielding her mouth with her hand, she has created an artificial chin rest to appear more natural. She would look bizarre if she went to any greater lengths to broadcast the need for privacy in the

communication. Her shoulders are slumped forward and neck craned to leave her face visible only to the person she is speaking to.

▶▶ Her blonde friend appears to touch her lower lid as she listens and is probably talking about the object of their discussion. Although eye probing is normally an adaptor, in this case it is a well-developed and practiced mask for speaking privately. As she puts her hand to her eye she shields her mouth, hiding those words from the object of the discussion—the couple to the right of the picture. Notice specifically the barrier location.

≫ Focus on the remaining woman in the back row. The woman appears to be there alone. She is not engaged in any of the conversation. She shows strong signs of needing more space, crossing her abdomen in the egg-protector pose. She also holds some object in front of her crotch though and appears to have a bag on her shoulder. She grips her wrist in a way that suggests an adaptor, and is either turned down right with her eyes or looking the other way to avoid the situation to her left.

≫ Focus on the two young men to her right. They appear to have found something interesting to discuss, and their focus follows whatever it is as their engagement stays with each other. Although little is discernable from the young man in the black suit, the other young man is crossing his torso with an arm and rubbing the opposite forearm with his hand—a classic male barrier-adaptor combo.

≫ Focus on the two women at the forefront and center of the group. Neither is directly facing the other in the conversation. They appear to be having a normal chat and they have the interviewers as their focus. Both are standing openly, but barriered. One is double-barriered, using the egg-protector pose and her over-garment to supplement. Both have rounded shoulders, which is probably their normal posture. They appear to be speaking openly and not about anything secretive. If they are discussing the younger couple, it is not evident.

>> Focus on the woman to the far left in the front row. She is caught up in thought. Her head drifts down to her as her right arm is in a lifeless hang. Even in this state of thought, she is barriering with her portfolio. This is purely unintentional messaging for the most part. Like the other two ladies in the front row, she points to the object that brings her here with her toes—that is, the interviewers. Her feet are almost surely touching at the heels based on the pie-shaped pattern between her toes in the front. This might well be a sophisticated adaptor or simply her normal posture.

>> Focus all the way in the back. Only a portion of a woman sitting is visible. She has arms tightly folded, indicating a need for more space and some kind of high-thought underway, whether intensely cognitive or emotional is difficult to tell.

>> Focus on the interviewers.

>> The man in the center is fidgeting with the cap to the Sharpie—clearly an adaptor. Perhaps he is just as uncomfortable as the interviewees. Who knows what happened in his home life, on the drive in, or what tape is playing in his head at the moment.

>> All three men are clearly anchored to their barrier (the desk), and in fact the one on the right cannot get the whole thing so he is willing to hide just one half of his body and to sacrifice comfort for it. The other two men are leaned forward to anchor to the barrier. The man on the right is fidgeting with a pen and has one hand in his uncovered lap as a form of barrier to make up for the diminished barrier of the table.

➤ The two men on the right appear to be in conversation and engaged, but without seeing the eyes it is difficult to know about engagement.

➤ The man on the left is clearly engaged in what is happening across the room with the couple.

What I have just done is a behavioral symptoms analysis. It takes into account ordinary elements of body language discussed in the handbook and overlays them onto given situations. The only way to truly know how accurate this is would be to ask all parties involved. That entails everyone there being honest, not only with you, but also with themselves.

Snapshots of daily life just like this present you with abundant opportunities to observe carefully. Sometimes you will even get a chance to take it to the next level and verify your assessment. You cannot know another person's thoughts using body language analysis, but you can approximate what the behavior means and give yourself a head start. That knowledge is powerful. Think about your own behavior and what you are signaling in a similar situation. Knowing what a trained eye can see, you can now build on that.

Conclusion

People are wonderfully complex and diverse, with some profound commonalities—not just commonalities in physiology and neurology, but, as a result of those, in drives, thoughts, and methods of communication.

The commonalities mean that there are only so many things we can possibly do with our hands feet, eyes, and bodies. The same could be said for finite numbers of sounds, and yet we have evolved millions of combinations of those sounds to create meaning.

As we have relied on these spoken messages, we have blunted all but the most primitive of signaling with our bodies. In customary human fashion, we have tried to overcome that by creating signaling to mean the same thing as groups of words. That has worked fine in a group that understands the words the signaling is supposed to embody.

When you leave that group, the same signaling that meant "fantastic idea" no longer carries the same meaning. In fact, it might have adopted quite a different meaning based on the words of the other tribe—like "insulting idea." These gestures mean that even our attempts to create universal communication fall far short of the mark.

Many people today want a clear and easy toolkit to know what something means; they want a sort of dictionary of body language in the same way we have English-to-Arabic dictionaries. If you have ever tried to translate using a phrasebook, much less a dictionary, you know how complicated that is. This book is intended to give you a crash course in the syntax and grammar of body language, and allow you to use the phrases of body language we have included to learn to communicate passively as well as actively. Along the way, we have included examples and insights to prevent you from learning false cognates, which occur when people make the assumption, "this always means that."

In addition to our commonalities, humans are complicated and diverse, made of many interactions and experiences. These two, basic sets of rules are imperative if you are to learn to understand body language instead of creating parlor tricks.

Rule Set One

These are the five factors resulting from nurturing that influence body language:

» Self-awareness.

» Sophistication.

» Personal style, or grooming.

» Situational awareness.

» A sense of others' entitlement and what is proper.

Rule Set Two

▶▶ Some imaging is intentional; some is not.

▶▶ Intentional messaging is tempered by threat.

▶▶ Intensity can override filters.

▶▶ The five factors affect all rules.

▶▶ Distinguish between intentional and unintentional messaging.

All of the tools and information in the book are useless if you cannot open your eyes and stop projecting what something means. At the same time, you must remember that, when you are studying human body language, you will be like Jane Goodall among the chimps, with one distinct disadvantage: You are one of the chimps and cannot separate yourself.

As you have seen with the case studies, the minute you interact, the difficulty level in understanding body language escalates markedly. Stay as centered and objective as possible by remembering that body language is not about absolutes, it is about baseline. You are not going to get it right every time, but you are going to get better as you observe and listen methodically. By doing so, you are creating a real capability to read body language, not do parlor tricks. Enjoy!

Same Pose, Different Meanings: A Model for Analysis

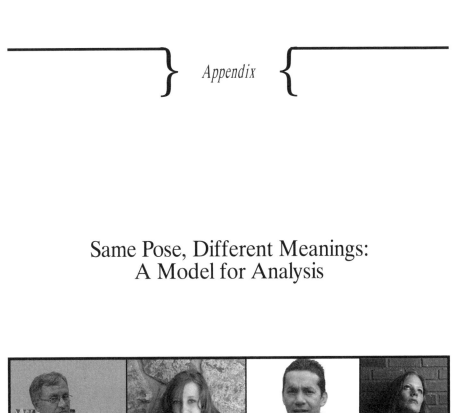

As you look at the photos, you need to consider context, gender, and how the arms are crossing the body. Assumptions about what it means to cross your arms or bite your lip will get you in trouble if you try to act on those assumptions. Understand the cause of actions, not the symptoms. Learn why people do things and what causes the body to do certain things, and pay attention to individual behavior.

Moving from left to right, notice first:

▶▶ The man's hands are completely tucked in.

▶▶ Only one of the young woman's hands is exposed.

▶▶ Both of the other man's hands are exposed.

▶▶ Only one of the other woman's hands is exposed.

Interpretation of the body language:

The man on the far left has his arms stacked in boredom. He is lounging (leaning back) and resting his arms in a pose that indicates he is waiting. His arms are unintentional and not meant to signal anything. They are relaxed; the hands are not gripping—simply stacked. The camera creates a bit of interest as stimulus. His eye contact is a response to the click of a shutter, so his eyes are open for data intake. Just seconds before the photo was taken, his eyes were focused down to the left in internal dialogue as he waits. If you add foot tap or finger drum, then the boredom becomes impatience.

Key in the young lady's messaging is the amount of engagement. She has absolute eye contact and a bit of disgust in her face. She is signaling negative body language, and the barrier is the mind's way of saying "off with you." The same amount of eye contact with a quizzical facial expression would signal uncertainty and timidity in the face of something she is interested in, but feeling vulnerable about. Her hands are exposed, with the overall demeanor being confrontational. There is a tremendous amount of judgment in the overall expression. She is engaged and focused with intentional negative signaling.

The second man shows folding of the arms and raised shoulder to indicate that he is less than confident in the situation. He has one hand poised as if he would like it to be free. His arms are being used as a barrier and eliminating or insulating from the threat. This man is inquisitive but feels unsafe. The grief muscle in his face drives home the message of uncertainty telegraphed by his rigid neck. He is interested in the object of his focus, but not certain he knows enough to want to engage. In this case, a barrier is most often unintentional signaling.

The second woman is clearly barriering to eliminate stimulus. She is sending an intentional message of "no more—I've had enough." Her eyes cast up and to the right are primarily to break eye contact, as though she is imagining life without you in it. She is past data-input mode. Her neck is stiff, her chin raised, and she is barriering with intent—a filter to prevent her from hearing what you are saying verbally or nonverbally.

Crossing the arms can simply be a comfortable position to sit, as in the first photo, or it can be a response to stimulus resulting in signaling. The first step is to look for intentional *versus* unintentional signaling.

Unintentional arm-crossing is typically a barrier intended to protect the person doing it, meaning that individual feels unsafe. Usually this kind of barrier is held closer and tighter and might include pinching of the shoulders or gripping tightly with the hands or arms. In either case, it involves tightening and less relaxation.

When intentionally using the arms to barrier, the aim is to block or eliminate the unwanted stimulus. This kind of signaling can be relaxed or tense, depending on the situation, but is never orchestrated with uncertain body language. The accompanying body language is always demonstrative and intended to send a signal.

Hidden hands mean the subjects are not signaling messages with them. The people with hands tucked in are not threatened; otherwise their hands would be exposed and ready for action. When someone exposes fingers, a profound amount of unintentional messaging is possible.

Use this model to do a similar analysis of common behavior that could have multiple interpretations, depending on whether it is intentional or unintentional, and on what other elements of body language accompany it. Two examples include sticking out the tongue and crossed legs.

Index

About the Authors

G REG HARTLEY's expertise as an interrogator first earned him honors with the U.S. Army. More recently, it has drawn national-level intelligence organizations and the international media to seek his insights about "how to" as well as "why."

He graduated from the U.S. Army Interrogation School, the Anti-Terrorism Instructor Qualification Course, the Principle Protection Instructor Qualification Course, and SERE (Survival, Evasion, Resistance, Escape) school.

His skills as an expert interrogator earned praise while he served as a SERE Instructor, Operational Interrogation Support to the 5th Special Forces Group during Operation Desert Storm, Interrogation Trainer, and as a creator and director of several joint-force, multinational interrogation exercises from 1994 to 2000. Among his military awards is the Knowlton Award. He attended law school at Rutgers University.

Greg has trained government agencies, private investigators, human resources representatives, and finance experts to read people and detect deception.

Hartley has provided expert interrogation analysis for major network and cable television, as well as National Public Radio and prime print media such as *The Washington Post* and *Philadelphia Inquirer*. Important foreign media such as BBC and *Der Spiegel* have also relied on his commentary. Hartley has contributed to articles for major magazines such as *Spin*, *Cosmopolitan*, *Marie Claire*, and *Details*.

Hartley created simulations of interrogation for British television in *Torture: The Guantanamo Guidebook*, and for the History Channel in *We Can Make You Talk*. Greg is featured in the Discovery Channel's *The Secrets of Interrogation* and contributed to the upcoming movie *Neurotypical*.

More recently Hartley has provided expert analysis of what people are really saying with behaviors and body language for national media like *Paula Zahn Now* and *Glenn Beck*. Hartley has made appearances on *The Montel Williams Show*, and countless news programs, local TV, and radio around the country.

MARYANN KARINCH is the author of 16 books, most of which address human behavior. She heads a literary agency and does coaching and presentations for corporate and academic audiences. Karinch and Hartley are coauthors of the best-selling titles *How to Spot a Liar*, *I Can Read You Like a Book*, and *Get People to Do What You Want*.